SJs

SPs

NFs

NTs

Temperament
and Parenting

By Larry Kidder

Please note: *This book combines ideas from these sources, reworked to remove contradictions and variations so that the materials are consistent and coherent. Illustrations and models are my own interpretations, unless otherwise specified.*

Sources:
www.themyersbriggs.com
kiersey.com
personalitymax.com
Jan Hackleman, The Family Connection
Wikipedia

If you are interested in hosting a temperament seminar, please contact:

Larry Kidder
lskidder@hotmail.com
909-227-9757

ISBN 978-1-387-74096-3

On the cover: *Temperament theory can be rather dull, dry, and boring. To lighten things up, I've used Keith Golay's portrayal of the four temperament families as animals, which represent the characteristics shown by each family group. There are **no other** insinuations or connotations to be made from the use of each animal beyond temperament theory.*

All content and design have been created by Larry Kidder. This book is self-published on Lulu.com.

Introduction

Parenting is the most important job in the world for which there is the least training and preparation. Once that pregnancy test comes back positive, first-time parents will likely feel a keen sense of inadequacy, lack of preparedness, and general panic—together with pure joy and wonder.

Those young first-time parents-to-be *who do not* feel the weight of responsibility are the couples for whom we should be most concerned.

This awesome responsibility represents the greatest characteristics we share with our Creator: we too are able to bring about new life—a rare gift indeed.

The transition from a married couple to a parental team represents far more than a positive pregnancy test. The success of the parental team rests entirely upon the relationship of the couple in the first place.

Getting that relationship right will set in motion the process of becoming a strong parental team able to withstand the rigors of parenthood.

Couples need to first learn to understand, tolerate, appreciate, and value the temperament of their parental partner. Only then will they be able to transfer that process to their children, establishing a warm, protected environment for their offspring.

The challenges of parenting were immediately felt by the First Family of humanity. Following their introduction to sin in the Garden of Eden, the young couple immediately set about establishing their new family.

Cain and Abel were the first human children. Adam and Eve had no human parents to model parenting—only God Himself. They were truly blazing a path for parenting that would stand for millennia to come.

How did things turn out? One son ended up murdering the other—not a very auspicious beginning. Sibling rivalry was the first of many family issues to cause conflict and tragedy for the human race.

As a parent, if your children successfully reach adulthood without murdering each other, you have already done better than the First Couple.

Seriously though, temperament theory gives you a major advantage in the arena of parenting. You will already know how to recognize the genetically based characteristics of your parental partner and your children. Rather than falling into the trap of trying to "fix" your spouse and your children, you will follow the path of understanding, tolerating, appreciating, and valuing human temperament-based differences.

The very process of learning and applying temperament theory takes the focus away from misunderstanding and judgment, and instead places it on understanding temperament differences and using that understanding to mutual advantage.

Human beings are surprisingly predictable. By identifying their temperaments, you will be able to not only anticipate their behaviors and reactions but you will learn tools to help manage their moods, making life better for everyone.

As a parent, you will benefit from some limited ability to predict your children's behavior and shape their personalities in healthy ways that correspond to their natural-born temperament characteristics.

However, talk to parents at various stages of family life and you will hear statements like, "Just when I figure my child out, he or she changes and enters a new growth phase."

A little predictability goes a long way in the practice of parenting. Knowing your child's temperament will help you preempt and manage behaviors and attitudes, using a variety of proven tools. Your knowledge of temperament will make you the smartest person in the room every time.

Human awareness of fundamental temperament differences is nothing new. In fact, a general awareness has been around for millennia.

One of the first to write about it was famed philosopher Hippocrates, who identified four fundamental temperament styles circa 450 B.C.

Those individuals who were more emotional and sensitive were labeled by Hippocrates as "choleric." Those who seemed more passive and detached he described as "phlegmatic."

More serious or even dour individuals he referred to as "melancholic." To the impulsive and excitable, he gave the label "sanguine."

Through the centuries since, the study of temperament has been expanded and developed by a host of philosophers, theorists, and researchers.

Carl Jung is perhaps the best-known psychologist to study and develop temperament theory, identifying outgoing people as extroverted and those more reflective and quiet as introverted.

In addition to extroverted versus introverted, which Jung referred to as the dominant difference between temperaments, he grouped these with thinking, feeling, sensation, and intuition.

His ideas inspired a famous mother-daughter duo to create the Myers-Briggs Type Indicator (MBTI), one of the premier tools used to determine temperament.

Katharine Cook Briggs and her daughter, Isabel Briggs Myers, developed four continua—or ranges—of human behavior to determine a four-letter label for MBTI-takers.

They identified four general groups: sensing and judging, or SJs; sensing and perceiving, or SPs; intuitive and feeling, or NFs; and intuitive and thinking, or NTs. Note that they expanded Jung's groupings to include judging and perceiving.[1]

These four families were further subdivided into four temperaments each, or 16 unique types: ESTJs, ISTJs, ESFJs, ISFJs, ESTPs, ISTPs, ESFPs, ISFPs, ENFJs, INFJs, ENFPs, INFPs, ENTJs, INTJs, ENTPs, and INTPs.

Many experts in psychology are able to remember their four-letter MBTI codes. Personally, I have taken the MBTI at least four times in my life and can only remember my two most recent results. I also recall that I was assigned different codes—INFJ and INTJ—probably because my mood and recent life experience at test time impacted my answers that day.

An aura of mystery surrounds the MBTI test for most people. Their answers must be analyzed and interpreted by professionals. In addition, the four-letter codes are easily forgotten because, for most of us, they are not useful or applicable to our daily lives.

Enter Keith Golay, PhD, a West Coast psychology professor, therapist, and author best known for his early theories regarding teaching and learning styles. A book he authored in 1982, titled *Learning Patterns and Temperament Styles,* is still widely used today, and primarily addresses the teaching and learning styles of

[1]https://www.truity.com/blog/how-psychologist-carl-jung-described-our-personality-types

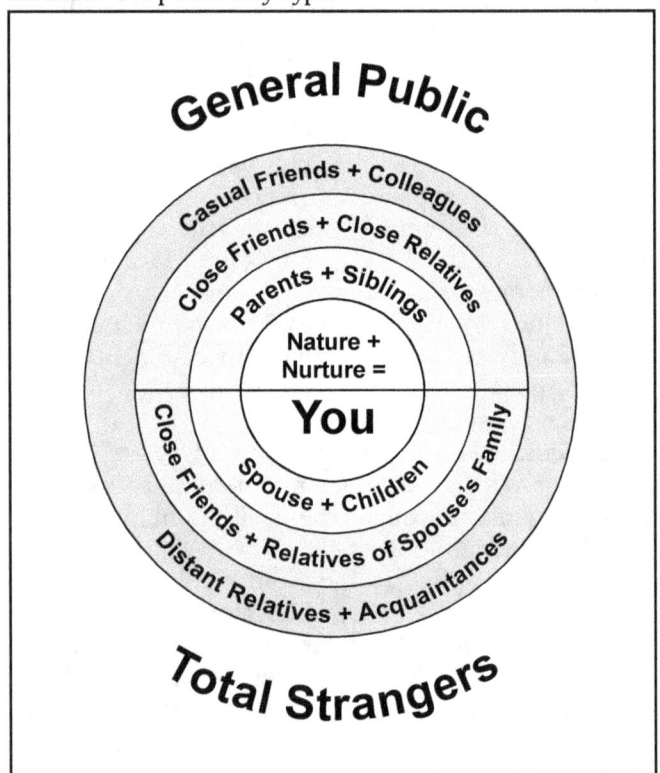

both music teachers and their students.

However, in a presentation he gave in 2002, titled "Introducing the Animal Kingdom—It's a Jungle Out There," Golay suggested four animals to represent the major temperament families: SJs, SPs, NFs, and NTs.[2]

Golay described the four groups as bears (SJs or guardians), apes (SPs or artisans), dolphins (NFs or idealists), and owls (NTs or intellectuals). The simple assignment of animals to the four temperament families immediately made the MBTI four-letter codes far more memorable and accessible to the layperson.

In this publication, I've studied the various temperament analogies available online, compared their approaches to temperament, and combined aspects from each into what I believe is a coherent approach, smoothing the many variations and contradictions into a unified theory.

I've adopted Golay's animal families. Unlike the MBTI, which is shrouded in mystery for the average test-taker, I am choosing to take readers on a personal journey of learning temperament theory and developing a level of expertise.

In my opinion, the power of temperament theory should not be limited to expert interpretation. Instead, it should provide a tool to help individuals better understand and accept themselves, and do the same for those around them. By far, the greatest diversity between human beings is found in temperament.

My purposes for preparing this book can be summed up by the following.

Understand, tolerate, accept, and ultimately value various human temperaments. I believe a majority of people have no concept of temperament theory. We do not choose our temperament any more than when and where we will be born.

Follow the process. Once people realize that temperament characteristics aren't good, bad, right, or wrong, they are able to switch into a mode of understanding, toleration, acceptance, and even appreciation of themselves and others.

A football team would be in deep trouble if its members were clones of each other. Teams, whether in the workplace, home, or elsewhere, are strengthened by the diversity of their members. Human beings are far more successful when the unique perspectives, talents, skills, and ideas of all temperaments are harnessed.

These tools and techniques are meant to be used and applied—over and over. They will shift the focus from self-judgment and other-judgment to self-acceptance and other-acceptance. *In my opinion, this could be world-changing and revolutionary.*

[2]*American Music Teacher,* Vol. 52, No. 2 (October–November 2002), pp. 40-44.

The Four Continua

Based on Carl Jung's four psychological functions of sensation, intuition, feeling, and thinking, the mother-daughter duo of Katharine Cook Briggs and Isabel Briggs Myers developed the following four continua or ranges:

- **Extroversion** (E) ⟷ **Introversion** (I)
- **Sensing** (S) ⟷ **Intuition** (N)
- **Thinking** (T) ⟷ **Feeling** (F)
- **Judging** (J) ⟷ **Perceiving** (P)

According to one source, Katherine Cook Briggs embarked on her research and study of temperament theory as a way to understand her son-in-law, Chief Myers, who was clearly "different" from the rest of the family. Seeking to be closer to her daughter, she chose to better understand and appreciate her son-in-law, rather than be critical and judgmental.

When she discovered the temperament theories of Carl Jung, she ceased developing her own system and adopted his ideas, expanding upon them. During her life, she was able to personally visit with Jung when he traveled to the United States.[1]

She and her daughter, who helped her develop the Myers-Briggs Type Inventory (MBTI), theorized that people land somewhere on each of these four continua, and where they fall determines their temperament.

It should be noted that few individuals land at either pole. Some may find themselves near the middle, making it more difficult to determine whether they favor one side or the other.

Those who find it difficult to choose a side may be experiencing certain realities related to temperament theory: 1) some temperaments struggle simply choosing and committing; 2) some temperaments have more difficulty with self-reflection or self-analysis; 3) some individuals have been told by others that certain temperament characteristics are wrong or bad; or 4) some people are truly a mix.

Those who complete the MBTI test are assigned a four-letter code, based on which side of each continuum they favor. For example, my most recent MBTI code was INFJ—suggesting that I am introverted, intuitive, feeling, and judging. However, I resonate more with the traits of INTJs and have been so identified by a previous MBTI test.

What would make temperament theory more memorable, reliable, and applicable to daily life? First, involve people in the process of determining their own temperaments by familiarizing them with the theories and concepts, and assisting them in applying the theories and concepts to their lives.

Second, find a more interesting and accessible way to describe the temperaments that is less mysterious and more fun (see the next chapter).

To begin with, here is a simplified discussion of temperament theory, based on the MBTI, with a number of definitions that are a compilation of multiple sources, smoothing out inconsistencies.[2]

Extroversion (E) vs. Introversion (I)

Let's begin with the continuum which is the most recognizable: extroversion versus introversion.

Extroverted individuals:
- Are described as outgoing and gregarious.
- Are comfortable working in groups, and are energized by the process and interactions.
- Prefer a wide range of friends, with a wider circle of acquaintances.
- May act impulsively, making quick decisions without fully considering the consequences.
- May be uncomfortable by themselves and with their own thoughts.

Introverted individuals:
- Are described as more reflective or reserved.
- Enjoy being by themselves or with a small group.
- Prefer to know a few people well.
- May spend too much time deep in thought and not take action.
- May not consider whether their thoughts and ideas are practical.

Most societies value extroversion over introversion. In fact, introverts are seen as shy, withdrawn, and socially inept (all negatives) while extroverts are described as outgoing and friendly (all positives).

However, some extroverts lack social filters, and can be rude and edgy, while some introverts are well able to switch into a gregarious mode as needed.

The key to determining whether someone is extroverted or introverted is found in where they go to recharge emotional reserves. Extroverts are energized by interacting with others, while introverts seek quiet and solitude to replenish their emotional reserves.

---

[1] https://www.truity.com/myers-briggs/story-of-mbti-briggs-myers-biography

[2] Temperament definitions in this publication represent the compilation of a variety of websites and other resources.

Sensing (S) vs. Intuition (N)

Sensing individuals focus on the physical environment—what can be seen, heard, touched, tasted, or smelled. They live "in the moment," experiencing what is present and real, and looking for practical applications of what they learn. Experience and action are preferable to words and ideas.

Intuitive individuals give more credence to impressions, meanings, and patterns when interpreting information and personal experience.

Sensing individuals:
- Recall events as snapshots of what has happened.
- Solve problems by gathering and focusing on facts.
- Pragmatically look for the bottom line.
- Trust experience over impression or interpretation.
- May struggle with or simply not care to see the big picture.
- May limit themselves by failing to consider all of the possibilities.

Intuitive individuals:
- Remember events based on their impressions and interpretations.
- Solve problems by considering a wide range of ideas and possibilities.
- Prefer innovation over the tried and true.
- See the big picture as a framework for details.
- Interpret their experiences, based on impressions.
- May be challenged when moving from ideas to action and reality.

Thinking (T) vs. Feeling (F)

In this third continuum, it's easy to confuse thinking with intelligence and feeling with emotion. Instead, this pairing looks more at how people approach decision-making.

Individuals who lean toward thinking base their decisions upon fundamental facts or precedent, regardless of the situation unfolding before them.

They also prefer the practical over theoretical, and often list the pros and cons before making a decision. They resist allowing their own or others' feelings and emotions to influence their decision process.

On the other hand, feeling individuals place greater emphasis upon what others care about, as well as their points of view and emotions.

Personal feelings influence their decision process, and they are intent on maintaining harmony.

Thinking individuals:
- Gravitate toward logic and science.
- Notice and point out inconsistencies.
- Look for logical explanations and solutions.
- Focus on what is fair or just.
- Value truth over tact.
- May be perceived as blunt and hurtful of the feelings of others.

Feeling individuals:
- Are people-focused.
- Value harmony and avoid conflict.
- Care deeply about the opinions, feelings, and well-being of others.
- Make decisions based on compassion and empathy.
- Choose tact over the cold, hard truth.
- May be perceived as idealistic, sentimental, or indirect.

Judging (J) vs. Perceiving (P)

The fourth and final continuum describes the polar opposites of judging and perceiving. Similar to the previous, this final continuum relates primarily to the process of and comfort with making decisions.

Some people are naturally able to make up their minds and stick to their decisions, while others struggle to come to a decision because of unknown consequences or many options. And, once they've made a decision, they continue to question their choices and worry about unanticipated outcomes.

Judging individuals approach the world in an orderly and structured fashion. They prefer to be settled and organized, keeping their environment controlled and predictable. But when things go awry, they seem better able to shrug their shoulders and say *c'est la vie* ("that's life" in French).

Perceiving individuals tend to rely on input from a variety of sources—sometimes too many—before coming to a decision.

They are perceived by others as open-ended, flexible, spontaneous, and eager for new experiences and information.

Judging individuals:
- Are driven to make decisions, feeling unsettled until they do.
- Are more task-oriented.
- Enjoy making lists and checking them off.
- Believe in work before play.
- Avoid procrastination.
- May rush the decision-making process.

Perceiving individuals:
- Stay open, flexible, and fluid.
- Are more casual and relaxed.
- Prefer minimal—if any—planning.
- Experience bursts of energy and creativity.
- May delay decisions, hoping for more input.

Extroversion  Introversion

- Talkative, outgoing
- Prefers a fast-paced environment
- Works through ideas with others
- Uncomfortable being alone
- Enjoys being center of attention

- Reserved, private
- Prefers slower, thoughtful pace
- Thinks through ideas
- Comfortable being alone
- Observes, avoids spotlight

Sensing  Intuition

- Focused on reality
- Pays attention to details and facts
- Prefers practical ideas
- Describes things in literal ways
- Is specific, clear

- Focused on impressions
- Pays attention to the big picture
- Prefers creative, innovative ideas
- Looks for meaning, patterns
- Uses concepts, interprets

Thinking  Feeling

- Logical, impersonal
- Values justice, fairness
- Notices inconsistencies
- Reasonable, level-headed
- Critical of people and ideas

- Decisions based on beliefs, values
- Impact of actions on others
- Values harmony, forgiveness
- Warm, empathic, tactful
- Pleases and supports others

Judging  Perceiving

- Prefers to have matters settled
- Respects rules and deadlines
- Prefers step-by-step instructions
- Carefully plans, prepares
- No surprises, please

- Leaves options open
- Rules and deadlines are flexible
- Improvises
- Enjoys surprises and new situations
- Spontaneous

Source: https://en.wikipedia.org/wiki/Myers%E2%80%93Briggs_Type_Indicator

Self-Analysis

☞You may think to yourself, "I identify with aspects from both sides of the continua. How do I choose?" However, characteristics on one side will *energize* you and feel totally natural, taking little if any effort. The other side will *sap* your emotional reserves and require you to recharge. For instance, I am able to improvise very well when needed, but I am exhausted afterwards. I like to know the score of a game before it's over so that I have no surprises. I have anxiety before I begin a test or game of chess—because I don't know the outcome and fear failure or embarrassment. I am more **Judging** than **Perceiving**.

What is Your Four-Letter Code?

Imagine that you are in a debate over which of the opposite poles is best and why. Which side is more natural for you to defend?

Both sides may seem right, but honestly choose which side feels more natural to you.

Parents, authority figures, siblings, colleagues, and even peers may tell you that your tendencies are wrong because they differ from theirs. The tendency of human beings to consider others as inferior, less intelligent, wrong, or bad because they are different is far too common *but is fundamentally flawed.*

If you're struggling to choose, ask someone who knows you well to help you answer. Certain aspects of self-reflection and personal discovery may seem challenging, but they are worth the effort. Keep in mind that indecisiveness is a tendency for some temperaments.

For each pair of statements below (left vs. right), choose either the left or right statement that best resonates with you. Resist the temptation to rely on what others—especially authority figures—may have told you in the past. But do ask someone who knows you well to help you answer if you're having trouble deciding. Remember, this is a journey!

Extrovert (E) vs. Introvert (I)

❑ I am naturally talkative and outgoing.	❑ I am naturally reserved and private.
❑ I enjoy an active, fast-paced environment.	❑ I enjoy a slower, more thoughtful pace.
❑ I work through ideas by discussing them with others.	❑ I work through problems and ideas in my head.
❑ I enjoy being part of a team, interacting and problem-solving together.	❑ I am more efficient when I work alone or with a small group of colleagues.
❑ I am comfortable being the center of attention.	❑ I'm uneasy when the spotlight turns on me.
❑ I tend to think out loud.	❑ My thoughts are a sanctuary.
❑ I am recharged by being around others.	❑ I seek out peace and quiet to recharge.

Sensing (S) vs. Intuition (N)

❑ I remember events as a series of scenes.	❑ I remember events based on my impressions.
❑ I focus on the here and now.	❑ I interpret the past and worry about the future.
❑ I tend to talk about everyday life.	❑ I tend to talk about abstract ideas or relationships.
❑ I pay attention to details and facts.	❑ I pay attention to my gut feelings and impressions.
❑ I am practical, looking at previous experiences to determine what to do next.	❑ I am creative and innovative, looking for possibilities and untried solutions.
❑ I describe life in literal ways through my five senses—sight, sound, smell, touch, and taste.	❑ I describe life through feelings, concepts, theories, ideas, illustrations, and metaphors.
❑ I prefer specific and practical thoughts and ideas.	❑ I search for meaning and purpose.

Thinking (T) vs. Feeling (F)

❏ I base decisions on pure logic and reason.

❏ I value justice and fairness.

❏ I look for inconsistencies in arguments.

❏ I am very bothered by hypocrisy.

❏ I see myself as level-headed and matter-of-fact.

❏ The truth is more important than people's feelings.

❏ I am comfortable with conflict.

❏ I base decisions on personal values and feelings.

❏ I value mercy and harmony.

❏ I support others and avoid criticizing them.

❏ I value forgiveness and avoid judging others.

❏ I see myself as warm and empathetic.

❏ Feelings are sometimes more important than truth.

❏ I avoid conflict whenever possible.

Judging (J) vs. Perceiving (P)

❏ I prefer to have matters settled.

❏ Rules and deadlines should always be respected.

❏ I prefer to have detailed, step-by-step instructions.

❏ I like to know what I'm getting into ahead of time.

❏ I avoid procrastination. I schedule my time so that I am not rushed at the end.

❏ I believe in work before play.

❏ I rely on lists.

❏ I prefer to leave my options open.

❏ Rules and deadlines should have flexibility.

❏ I like to figure things out as I go along.

❏ I relish the unexpected.

❏ I've sometimes procrastinated, especially when making tough decisions or dealing with conflict.

❏ I believe that work and play can be mixed.

❏ Operating without a list gives me more flexibility.

Now it's time to interpret your results. Consider these as a starting point. We are following a process with multiple approaches designed to not only help you sort out your temperament but fully integrate these concepts into your daily life.

A challenge for the MBTI—or any self-reporting tool for that matter—is the unpredictability of moods for many human beings, who may feel differently from day to day.

On a given day, I believe that my results could reflect my current mood, recent experiences, or a host of other factors. I have taken the MBTI on multiple occasions and received different results.

The process I follow in this book includes several questionnaires *and* information regarding temperament theory, hoping you will intuitively come to a conclusion about your natural characteristics that will aid you in understanding yourself and how you relate to others.

To interpret this exercise, complete the following steps and report them below:

1. Tally each of the four continua. Compare the numbers under each section to see where you land.
2. The greater the difference between the left and right, the more pronounced your leanings.
3. A simple majority will provide an MBTI code. Even if it's close, write in your scores below. Your code may or may not be supported by what you learn in the following pages, but you will have ample opportunities to refine your results as we continue.

E__ I__   S__ N__   T__ F__   J__ P__

(drum roll…) ☐ ☐ ☐ ☐

Bears, Apes, Dolphins, and Owls

The Myers-Briggs and Golay merger results in the following four families of temperaments and their specific types. **Bears** *(sensing + judging, or SJ)* account for 41 percent of the population, according to one statistical model, making this the largest temperament group in the world. **Apes** *(sensing + perceiving, or SP)* are second at 33 percent. **Dolphins** *(intuition + feeling, or NF)* are third at 14 percent. **Owls** *(intuition + thinking, or NT)* are the rarest temperament family, coming in at just 12 percent of the population.[1]

While these numbers may vary slightly across geography, culture, race, and socioeconomic classes, temperament is by far the single most consistent determinant of fundamental diversity between human beings—far more than culture, race, or even gender.

Statistical variations around the world are more likely to be caused by persecution and alienation of those with independent tendencies by the ruling classes. In more totalitarian countries, freedom-seeking and creative temperaments that resist or question dictatorial or party rule are simply eliminated!

Bears (SJs)
Stabilizers and Guardians

The four bear temperaments share sensing (S) and judging (J). At approximately 41 percent of the population, *bears rule the world.*

They are most interested in membership and productivity—belonging to and contributing to groups and organizations. They value responsibility, accountability, predictability, security, and stability.

Bears are dutiful and loyal, supporting institutions by setting up and enforcing policies and procedures. They value acts of duty and service.

In the wild, mother bears in particular are protectors of their cubs, standing guard in the face of any threat—including the larger male bears. Many hikers have learned that they should never find themselves between a mother bear and her cubs, or they risk serious injury and even death.

Tradition and history are valued and celebrated by those with bear temperaments, and they feel responsible for acculturating the generations to follow in such important matters.

---

[1]https://personalitymax.com/personality-types/temperaments/

As concrete thinkers, bears operate in the realm of what is known and accepted, living in the here and now.

Status is very important to bears. With status comes guaranteed loyalty and allegiance. Hierarchy is to be respected and honored, and authority is to be obeyed without question by *all* temperaments.

As students, bears prefer structure and predictability, exemplified by the traditional lecture and exams. Their orientation to detail leads them to take careful notes and memorize facts, from which they hope to construct an overarching global understanding. However, many bears never come to see the big picture, relying entirely upon facts and details.

Since duty and responsibility are so highly valued, the worst thing a bear can do is fail at duties or responsibilities. Admission of shortcomings of any kind suggests failure, and bears typically have a difficult time admitting failure or ignorance of any kind.

They *must* be right.

Apes (SPs)
Performers and Artisans

The four ape temperaments share sensing and perceiving. At 33 percent of the population, apes value freedom above all else, insisting on choosing their next actions, as well as looking for impact and results. Apes hope to be seen as graceful,

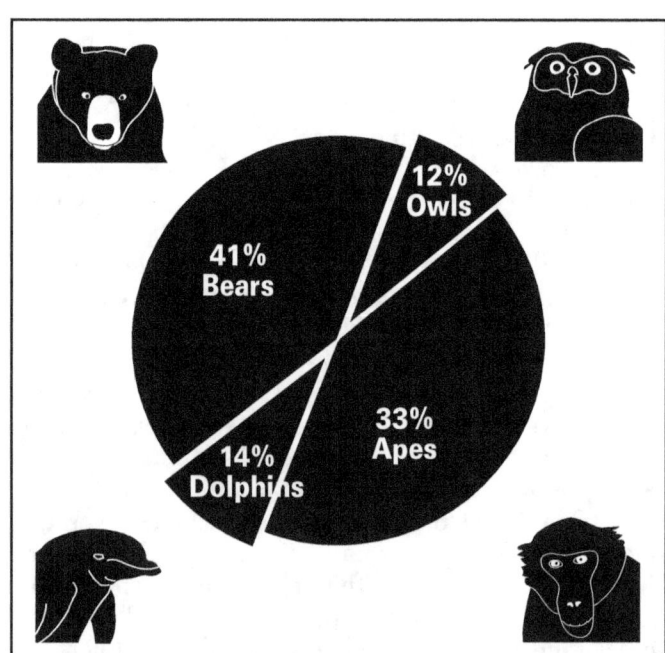

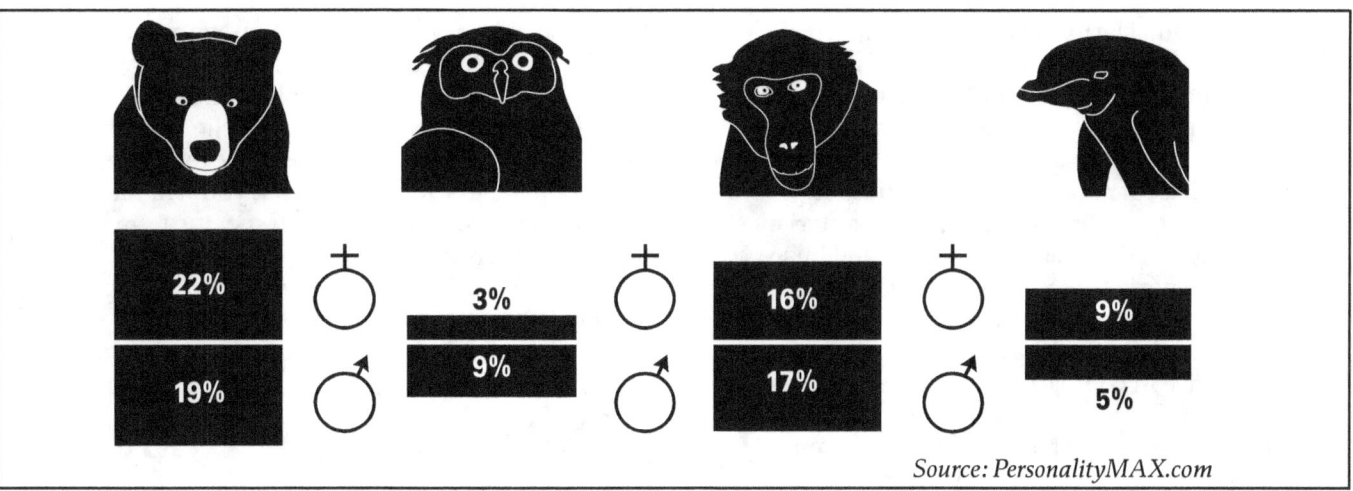

22%   ♀
3%   ♀   16%   ♀   9%
19%   ♂   9%   ♂   17%   ♂   5%

Source: PersonalityMAX.com

adept, skillful, bold, and impressive.

The phrase, "the ends justify the means," was likely coined by an ape or used to describe one.

Generally optimistic and energetic, apes are absorbed by immediate action in the concrete present. They seek adventure and stimulation.

Spontaneity, impulse, serendipity, and the ability to quickly assess and solve problems they encounter are highly valued and respected personally and in others.

Apes love games, relying on their skills, instincts, and quick reflexes. Parties and festivities excite extrovert apes, and quiet heroism the introverts. As instinctive negotiators, some are skilled with seizing opportunities and making tactical moves that lead to impressive results. While other temperaments may freeze in the face of imminent danger, apes spring into action.

Artisan apes are naturally gifted with their hands, creating masterpieces or solving mechanical or technological problems. They pull from many resources, accomplishing impressive solutions.

However, a general warning by apes: *Don't stand in the way of progress.*

Dolphins (NFs)
Catalysts and Idealists

At 14 percent of the population, dolphins focus primarily on relationships—knowing and being known.

The four dolphin temperaments share intuition and feeling.

Dolphins are benevolent and empathetic, valuing human identity, meaning, and significance. They particularly prize openness and authenticity.

Described by others as idealists and visionaries, dolphins tend to be optimistic about the future. They trust their abilities to interpret and relate both verbally and nonverbally with those around them. They are especially concerned with making everyone feel wel-

comed, accepted, and included.

Dolphins are driven by their need to find a purpose, working toward a greater, common good. They seek a unique and authentic identity.

As students and colleagues, dolphins function best when they are able to relate to their fellow students, teachers, workers, and bosses on a personal level.

Along with their desire for unity and inclusion, they bring a diplomatic skillset, searching for common beliefs and experiences, drawing people together by finding shared purposes and goals.

Their need for authenticity leads them to focus on ethics and morality—with integrity as a priority.

However, they draw the line when they see others being mistreated. *They will step in and intercede.*

Owls (NTs)
Theorists and Rationalists

As the rarest of the temperaments, owls comprise just 12 percent of the population. The four owl temperaments share intuition and thinking. At just one percent each, mastermind owls and counselor dolphins have the distinction of being the least common temperaments.

Above all else, owls value knowledge, competency, and mastery. They learn all they can, then question the validity and reliability of what they've learned.

Owls are fascinated by the world and seek to understand the how and why. They critique what they see, believing that improvements can and should be made. The very fact that an idea is well-established is reason enough to give it closer examination. Rules, policies, regulations, and even traditions are conditional and fluid. They can find an exception to every rule.

Owls trust logic and reason, possessing a healthy skepticism and seeking to define, categorize, structure, and reorganize their world.

Precision and clarity are of utmost importance—especially when it comes to thought and language.

Owls tend to be the most critical temperament family, looking for ways to improve themselves and others. Their criticism is particularly annoying to bears, along with a lack of natural respect for authority.

Owls possess a number of unique characteristics and skills, such as the ability to visualize and imagine various scenarios, plan ahead, invent, and design. Because they spend much time in their own thoughts, they may struggle in the area of social skills.

Owls thrive in complexity and chaos, quickly assessing their environment and setting out to reorganize it better than before. They are driven to problem-solve as well as develop theories, models, and principles to be applied to future situations.

But beware: *Owls will likely believe they are smarter than other temperaments.*

Concrete vs. Abstract

Bears and apes are concrete, while dolphins and owls are abstract. This is primarily shown through their communication styles and thought processes.

Concrete communicators focus on everyday experiences and observations, while abstract communicators prefer ideas, concepts, theories, and hypotheses.

Concrete temperaments may find abstract conversations boring and tedious. On the flipside, abstract temperaments often find concrete conversations mundane and superfluous.

This fundamental disconnect can lead to major relational and communication issues.

Cooperative vs. Utilitarian

Bears and dolphins are cooperative by nature. They are more concerned about doing the right thing, treating people well, and being liked.

Apes and owls are utilitarian by nature. They are more interested in finding out what works and less worried about the impact of their decisions and actions on others.[2]

To Which Temperament Family Do You Belong?

In Exercise 1, you began the process of determining your four-letter MBTI code. Now it's time to apply what you've learned about the four temperament families and see how your code holds up.

You are looking for patterns that will identify you with one of the following families: SJ (bears), SP (apes), NF (dolphins), or NT (owls). What you learn about each of these families, together with what you already know about yourself, will help you identify with your

family group—bears, apes, dolphins, or owls.

In the first exercise, you worked to pinpoint where you land on each of the four polar continua. In the following exercise, you will approach the identification process by looking for patterns of beliefs with which you resonate. In the next chapter, you will find the unique characteristics of the 16 specific temperaments to help further refine your self-identification.

Remember: relationships exist where temperament and environment intersect and collide. Like the humans involved, each relationship is complex and unique.

Potential Pet Peeves
How each may view
the other temperament families

Bears may see ...

Apes as lazy, disrespectful, rebellious
Dolphins as sappy, lenient, emotional
Owls as conceited, disrespectful, aloof

Owls may see ...

Bears as simple-minded, bossy, stuck
Dolphins as too caring, forgiving, nosy
Apes as impulsive, shallow, chaotic

Apes may see ...

Bears as inflexible, obstructive
Dolphins as boring, gullible
Owls as geeky, physically clumsy

Dolphins may see ...

Bears as uncaring, unbending, arbitrary
Apes as impulsive, self-centered
Owls as hypercritical, socially clumsy

---

[2]https://keirsey.com/temperament-overview/

	Concrete Thinkers Sensing (S) | Prefer Tangible World		**Abstract Thinkers** Intuitive (N) | Prefer Ideas, Concepts	
	Bears 41% Caretakers Judging Close-ended	**Apes 33%** Users Perceiving Open-ended	**Dolphins 14%** Heart Feeling Subjective	**Owls 12%** Mind Thinking Objective
Central Motivation	Responsibility	Freedom	Relationships	Competence
Primary Desire	To Serve	To Have Impact	To Know and Be Known	To Know More
Self Image	Doing a Good Job	Person of Action	Caring, Authentic	Smart, Competent
Craves	Recognition for Hard Work	Sensory Stimulation	Love and Understanding	Knowing the Unknown
Communicates Under Stress	Blames, Plays Victim	Non-verbal, Annhilates	Placates, Begs	Non-verbal, Debates
Wants to Know	What?	When? Where?	Who?	Why?
Greatest Fears	Irresponsibility, Disrespect	Loss of Freedom, No Impact	Seen as Uncaring, Insensitive	Failing, Looking Stupid
Teaching Style	Lectures, Structured	Demonstrates, Hands-on	Discusses, Group Interaction	Lectures, Probing Questions
Learning Style	Concrete, Routine	Concrete, Spontaneous	Abstract, Global	Abstract, Specific
Views Authority	Respects, Compliant	Challenges, Non-compliant	Pleases, Compliant	Challenges, Questions, Criticizes
Respects	Status, Position, Authority, Pedigree	Strength, Talent, Skill	Authenticity, Transparency	Knowledge, Competence, Strategy
Decisions Based Upon	Rules, History, Traditions	Instinct, Impressing Others	Intuition, Impact on Others	Logic, Strategy, Analysis
When Stressed	Complains	Retaliates	Becomes Confused, Forgets	Obsesses
Mental Pathologies	Psychosomatic, Depression	Raging, Addictions	Dissociation, Eating Disorders	Phobias, Obsessions
Personality Disorders	Passive-agressive, Borderline	Narcisistic, Antisocial	Histrionic, Borderline	Obsessive-compulsive, Avoidant
Leadership Styles	States Rules, Gives Cautions	Leads by Example, Takes Over	Facilitates, Suggests, Praises	Strategizes, Shares
Teaching Emphasis	Teacher-centered	Project-centered	Learner-centered	Content-centered

Source: Jan Hackleman, The Family Connection; minor changes by Larry Kidder

What is Your Temperament Family?

Multiple choice: Circle the letter of the phrase that best resonates with you. *Compel yourself to choose.* If you are an introvert, you are not as likely to speak up or take action yourself. However, you may support someone else speaking up or taking such actions on your behalf. If needed, ask someone who knows you to help you answer accurately.

1. I believe that rules and policies:

    B. (Bear)   Are to be followed out of respect for authority, history, and tradition.

    A. (Ape)   Can get in the way of progress or thwart successful action.

    D. (Dolphin)   Are there to help us get along with each other and avoid conflict.

    O. (Owl)   Are meant to be questioned, tested, criticized, and improved.

2. I believe authority figures should be:

    B. Respected because of their position or rank.

    A. Challenged or ignored, especially when they get in the way of progress or action.

    D. Seen as people worth getting to know and getting along with.

    O. Critiqued and held accountable for their mistakes, actions, or inaction.

3. When anticipating an event, I am *most* interested in knowing:

    B. What will take place.

    A. When and where it will take place.

    D. Who will be there.

    O. Why it is taking place.

4. Those I respect most are:

    B. Responsible and trustworthy—protectors of our society, culture, traditions, history, and institutions.

    A. People of skill and action, who know how to get things done.

    D. People who are warm, caring, transparent, and authentic.

    O. People who are knowledgeable, competent, logical, and intelligent.

5. I feel most fulfilled when I:

    B. Serve others around me and keep the world secure.

    A. Change the world for the better.

    D. Help others meet or exceed their potential.

    O. Organize chaos and find better solutions to problems.

6. In sports, I am most impressed by:

    B. Athletes who understand, respect, and follow the rules as well as the guidance of the coach.

    A. Athletes who are in excellent condition and highly skilled in their sport.

    D. Athletes who are emotionally connected to and supportive of their teammates.

    O. Athletes who are not only competent and skilled, but are able to out-think their opponents.

7. When I am threatened by others:

    B. I cite the rules and inform an authority figure.

    A. I fight back and protect myself with words and actions.

    D. I look for ways to make peace and find common ground.

    O. I develop strategies to protect myself and retaliate smartly if needed.

8. In the classroom:

    B. I enjoy listening to lecturers who teach in an organized manner and test in a predictable way.

    A. I prefer to watch a demonstration and learn by observing, then try it out for myself.

    D. I enjoy interacting with my classmates and teacher.

    O. I enjoy open-ended lectures, deep and weighty discussions, and problem-solving.

9. I am most impressed by:

    B. People of position and status.

    A. Strong, brave, and talented people.

    D. People who are willing to be open and honest.

    O. People who are highly competent, logical, and strategic.

10. As a leader, I would:

    B. Emphasize and enforce policies, rules, and guidelines, as well as demand respect.

    A. Lead by example and be willing to do any job I ask of those I supervise.

    D. Help those I lead to achieve personal and professional potential, then recognize their progress.

    O. Develop and communicate successful strategies to move the organization forward.

11. When I make decisions, I rely on:

    B. What has been tried and shown to work (why reinvent the wheel?).

    A. My ability to think on my feet and stay in the moment.

    D. My intuition and sense for what's best for everyone impacted.

    O. My ability to consider all scenarios, then pick the best way forward based on knowledge and logic.

12. I strive to be:

    B. A responsible worker and good citizen.

    A. A person of action and impact.

    D. A warm, caring, and authentic individual.

    O. A smart, logical, and competent person.

13. I prefer situations that are:

    B. Predictable and safe.

    A. Spontaneous and exciting.

    D. Relational and friendly.

    O. Challenging and complex.

14. In relating to others, it is most important for me to be:

    B. Fair and honest.

    A. Skilled and adaptable.

    D. Sensitive and tactful.

    O. Logical and knowledgeable.

15. I benefit others most by:

    B. Helping them learn history, culture, and social norms.

    A. Helping them learn skills, adaptability, and flexibility.

    D. Helping them relate better to others.

    O. Helping them apply knowledge and strategy to new situations.

16. It is my duty to:

    B. Follow the rules, set an example, and respect those in authority.

    A. Have a positive impact wherever I go.

    D. Help people get to know and understand each other better.

    O. Ensure that people and organizations function more logically and efficiently.

17. In a committee meeting:

    B. I remind my colleagues what has worked before, as well as rules and policies that guide our decisions and actions.

    A. I urge others to take action, even it challenges rules and policies—which may need to evolve.

    D. I am concerned about the ways our decisions and actions will impact the lives of others.

    O. I look for strategies and options, considering and testing a variety of hypothetical scenarios.

18. As a mentor in a corporate setting:

    B. I seek to help younger colleagues understand the structure, tradition, and guidelines that allow an organization to operate and thrive.

    A. I want to encourage young people to be bold and take action, changing their organization and their world for the better.

    D. I want to get to know my younger colleagues and have them know me, mentoring them in their new experiences and providing counsel that helps them be more successful.

    O. I want to encourage young professionals to question and respectfully challenge the *status quo,* being sure that logic and knowledge prevail in decision-making and strategy.

19. As a young artist:

    B. I colored within the lines.

    A. I colored with creativity and abandon.

    D. I enjoyed coloring with friends and classmates.

    O. I needed a good reason to color, then proceeded with competence.

20. I react to conflict by:

    B. Reminding people of the rules and guidelines, and how they help maintain order.

    A. Letting issues work themselves out so that people become stronger and tougher.

    D. Working hard to help people see multiple points of view and value each other.

    O. Discussing the issues and talking them through, finding answers that solve problems.

21. When looking at a problem:

    B. I want to know what has been done before.

    A. I want to try out different solutions and see how they work.

    D. I want to work together to find common ground and ideas that serve everyone.

    O. I want to consider all scenarios and choose the most logical plan of action.

22. As a member of a workplace team:

    B. I want to belong and know the goals up front.

    A. I want to know the limiting factors and what actions can be taken.

    D. I want to identify the strengths of my teammates and work together.

    O. I want to gather knowledge, explore, consider possibilities, and make smart decisions.

23. At parties and large gatherings:

    B. I enjoy belonging and socializing with friends and colleagues.

    A. I like telling fun, impressive stories, or participating in activities that require skill.

    D. I enjoy making new friends and getting to know my existing friends or colleagues better.

    O. I seek out other intellectuals who enjoy deep, meaningful discussions.

24. When I travel to new places:

    B. I am careful to learn and respect the rules of that culture so that I can blend in.

    A. I enjoy one-of-a-kind exciting and adventurous activities, as well as great cuisine and art.

    D. I enjoy meeting people and making new friends from other cultures.

    O. I enjoy learning about local history and culture, as well as understanding why they live their lives
       the way they do.

25. When doing a project:

    B. I begin by reviewing the guidelines and what others have done to accomplish similar tasks.

    A. I enjoy the process, being as creative and experimental as possible.

    D. I enjoy working with a group and taking part in the process.

    O. I strategize, choose the best process, work competently, then critique my results.

Now, tally your results to find how many bear, ape, dolphin, and owl statements with which you resonate. Keep in mind that some temperaments naturally find it more difficult to come to a decision. Others are not as well tuned to their feelings. The process of deciphering your temperament will provide you with important insights.

 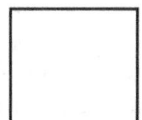  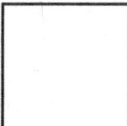  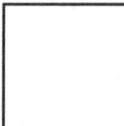  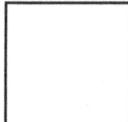

In Conclusion

There are three likely scenarios: 1) you see a clear dominance emerging of one temperament family; 2) you are a strong mix between two temperament families, with one slightly more pronounced; or 3) no clear winner has emerged.

If you are still unclear, keep working through the process. To be successful, you must identify and let go of the influences of others who have tried to change you into their image. Many truly believe they can change others—spouses, children, friends, colleagues. Truth is, we can only change ourselves. Ironically, others around us will evolve and change in relation to us.

Above all, accept that your temperament is neither right nor wrong, neither good nor bad. You are just the way you are. However, that does not excuse you from creating workarounds—strategies to overcome natural tendencies that threaten your ability to live and thrive in a world dominated by bears.

By identifying who you really are deep down, you will gain amazing insights into your instincts and natural tendencies, learning to love and accept yourself.

Along the same lines, you will understand how others are different than you to their very core, *and those differences are truly a blessing.*

The process will be challenging. Most people are uncomfortable scrutinizing their fundamental motivations and tendencies. They may not like what they see—probably because authority figures or peers have criticized, belittled, and confused them.

This book is designed to help you discover who you really are, accept yourself as you are, discover more about those around you, and accept them as they are.

Perhaps if people around the world would apply these principles, we would experience mutual respect, world peace, and prosperity.

For now, my primary goal is empower you with the tools of temperament theory so you can positively impact those within your sphere of influence.

The Sixteen Temperaments

Identifying your specific temperament is where the fun begins. Do the math and you will quickly realize that four families, each with four combinations, equate to 16 specific temperaments.

In Exercise 1, you determined a potential four-letter MBTI code for yourself. In Exercise 2, you explored temperament families and made a preliminary determination to which family you belong.

The four temperament families can be summed up in the following ways: Bears *guard and protect*. Apes *act and impact*. Dolphins *relate and mentor*. And owls *think and innovate*.

Most conflict in our world takes place because the various temperaments do not understand and respect each other. The potential "Pet Peeves" on page 10 suggest some possible ways each temperament family may view the other families.

Ask a husband or wife to list the things he or she would change about the spouse if given the opportunity. Ironically, *we think* we want others to believe and behave like we do. Yet, the world would be exceedingly dull and dysfunctional if we were all clones.

In the workplace, employees develop opinions and ideas regarding their colleagues that can enhance or disrupt the work environment. Those colleagues who resonate with their views, opinions, and ways of operating are considered more intelligent and skilled, while others who differ may be seen as adversarial or stupid.

Human beings are typically under the impression that they can change others. Parents, siblings, spouses, friends, acquaintances, colleagues, teachers, bosses, judges, and society at large attempt to change others through intimidation, guilt, or shame. They may temporarily coerce "change" out of others, but long-term and lasting change must be a personal choice.

As you consider the specific temperaments, keep in mind that you may not entirely identify with the characteristics shared here. Not a problem! You are looking for the temperament that most closely describes you.

The Bears (SJs – 41 percent)

Since our world is dominated by bears, we will begin by looking at this family, which shares sensing (S) and judging (J), and varies in introversion (I) vs. extroversion (E) and thinking (T) vs. feeling (F).

Remember, sensing individuals focus on reality, paying careful attention to concrete facts and details, preferring ideas that lead to practical applications, and describing things in specific, literal terms.

Judging individuals prefer to have matters settled, rules and deadlines respected, step-by-step detailed instructions given, and no surprises.

The four specific bear temperaments include Supervisors (ESTJ), Providers (ESFJ), Inspectors (ISTJ), and Protectors (ISFJ).

Supervisor Bears (ESTJ – 13 percent)

At 13 percent of the population, supervisor bears represent the single most prevalent temperament. Therefore, you are more likely to *be one or know one*. Your understanding of their natural tendencies will help you relate to them with more success.

Like their name suggests, supervisor bears prefer *to supervise*. With their extroverted nature, they need little if any prodding to step in and lead. Businesses, corporations, schools, charities, governments—virtually any organization will have its share of supervisor bears.

These individuals are typically generous with their time and service-oriented, faithfully attentive and willing to put in long volunteer hours as loyal members of service clubs, associations, and other groups.

Supervisor bears instinctively take charge and are comfortable giving orders. Cooperative with their superiors and colleagues, they expect those under their leadership to likewise show them the same respect and spirit of cooperation.

Rank and status are highly valued, and they take their obligations very seriously, as well as the privileges

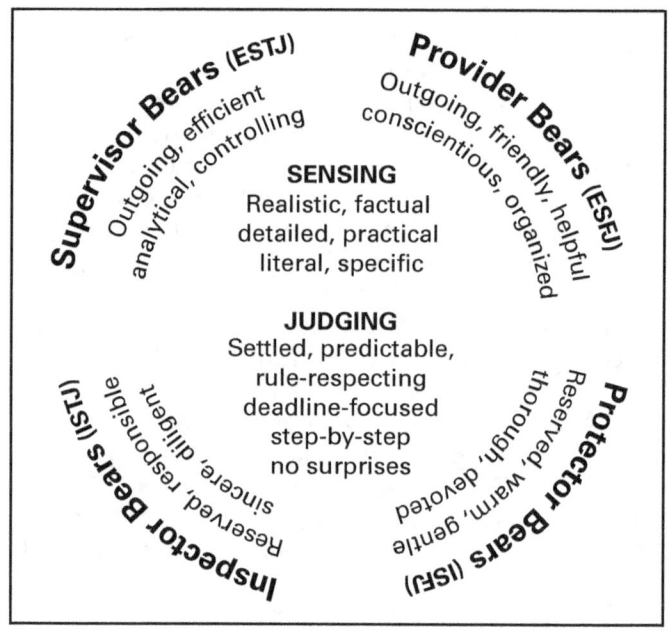

Supervisor Bears (ESTJ)
Outgoing, efficient analytical, controlling

Provider Bears (ESFJ)
Outgoing, friendly, helpful conscientious, organized

SENSING
Realistic, factual detailed, practical literal, specific

JUDGING
Settled, predictable, rule-respecting deadline-focused step-by-step no surprises

Inspector Bears (ISTJ)
Reserved, responsible sincere, diligent

Protector Bears (ISFJ)
Reserved, warm, gentle thorough, devoted

that should rightfully accompany rank and status.

Schedules, lists, agendas, and inventories are natural tools for them, and they prefer to stick to the tried and true rather than waste time experimenting. Firmly grounded and hardworking, they expect their subordinates to follow their example.

They do not hesitate to evaluate the performances of others, based on compliance and respect for rules, procedures, standards, and schedules. They are careful to give out praise—perhaps because they feel that others should be just as responsible and dutiful without needing or requiring external praise.

Their sense of responsibility and duty drives every aspect of their lives. They find it particularly difficult to accept criticism from others, perhaps because that would suggest they have failed in some way.

Supervisor bears tend to have a wide circle of friends and acquaintances. They look forward to ceremonies and social gatherings that celebrate traditions and history. Holiday parties, weddings, class reunions, award banquets, and other formal events are particularly gratifying.

They are direct in their conversations, which may seem harsh or condescending to those more sensitive. But they seldom, if ever, knowingly send mixed messages. Beware: *they must ultimately be in control.*

Provider Bears (ESFJ – 12 percent)

Equally social and outgoing as supervisor bears, provider bears represent the second most common temperament. They are driven to ensure the prosperity of their loved ones and friends.

They nurture social institutions such as schools, churches, clubs, and civic groups. Friendly social service comes naturally. They freely give of their time and energy to serve the needs of others through charitable work and volunteerism.

Provider bears are excellent team members, detailed and caring, good at logistics, and naturally stepping into leadership roles—or deferring to others as needed. Their spirit of leadership also translates into social gatherings, and they shine as masters of ceremony and hosts. They find it easy to speak and interact in public settings.

They are interested in their friends' lives and can chat pleasantly about virtually any concrete topic that is introduced. They particularly enjoy sharing good times and memories of years past.

While they are more sensitive to the feelings and needs of others than supervisor bears, they also find it difficult to accept criticism and are easily wounded. On the flipside, they are energized by praise and appreciation. Loving and affectionate, they seek and crave the same in return.

Out the total population, one quarter of all the people you will meet will be either a supervisor or provider bear. Face it: *bears rule the world.*

Inspector Bears (ISTJ – 9 percent)

The first of two introverted bears, inspector bears serve as the quiet guardians of institutions and organizations. They willingly accept their responsibilities, as well as the policies and procedures handed down to them by the leaders above. They are particularly critical and unaccepting of those who question or fail to adhere to the rules—no matter the reason.

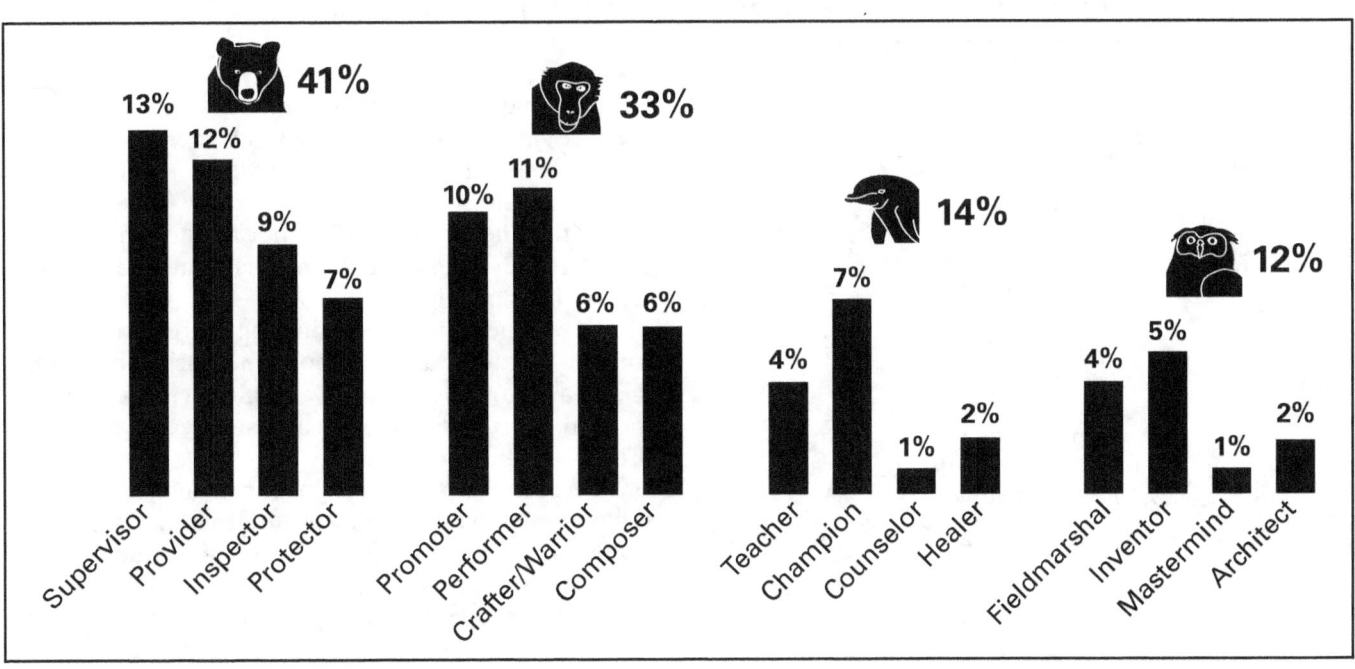

Inspector bears would likely be described by others as "super dependable," whether at home or in the workplace. They persevere in a dutiful and dedicated manner, keeping an eye on those under their supervision who are expected to follow suit. As introverts, they instinctively shy away from the spotlight.

Quality assurance is a priority, both with assignments and with people. Inspector bears are unyielding about the rules and guidelines. Other temperaments may misunderstand their primary motivation of duty. Similar to supervisors, they tend to be controlling.

Supportive of tradition, they are willing to take on leadership roles on occasion, particularly when such roles allow them to guide the next generation, and pass on skills and cultural history.

Shyness is revealed, though, when the gathering becomes too large, which can include birthdays, weddings, and anniversaries. They also become quite uncomfortable when the environment is too lavish or ostentatious, preferring the simple and down-to-earth. Their fashion style tends to be simple and conservative—and probably not a priority.

Protector Bears (ISFJ – 7 percent)

These introverted bears are motivated by the need to protect family, friends, coworkers, students, patients, and others for whom they feel responsible.

Protector bears have a strong sense of loyalty and responsibility, going out of their way to shield others from real and perceived dangers. Time-honored and time-trusted ideas and procedures are far safer.

Rules should be consistent and stable, as well as universally accepted and followed. Traditions and culture are to be protected and shared with the gener-

ations to follow, which are expected to enthusiastically embrace them. Status due to birth, title, office, or credentials is highly regarded and respected. Family histories, values, and objects are cherished and maintained.

Warm-hearted and sympathetic, protector bears champion the downtrodden and are willing to sacrifice unselfishly for the good of others.

However, their shy and reserved style can be perceived by others as stiff or cold.

Protector bears are typically hardworking, happy to do the chores and tasks that others consider beneath them, and content to work tirelessly by themselves.

They are thorough and frugal, valuing and tracking every cent and criticizing those who squander. Conscientious, they follow through until a task is completed.

All of these characteristics can lead to overwork and under-appreciation, and others may take advantage of their diligence and generosity.

The Apes (SPs – 33 percent)

Apes represent the second largest temperament family. As a group, they are the most likely to take action as well as become irritated with inaction—particularly when someone impedes progress.

They share sensing (S) and perceiving (P). As sensing individuals, they live in the moment, experiencing life though their five senses. As perceiving, they thrive in uncertainty and prefer to leave their options open. They are also spontaneous and improvisational.

Apes vary in extroversion (E) vs. introversion (I), and thinking (T) vs. feeling (F).

The four specific ape temperaments include Promoters (ESTP), Performers (ESFP), Crafter/Warriors (ISTP), and Composers (ISFP).

Promoter Apes (ESTP – 7 percent)

Life is never dull around promoter apes. They are people of action. And when they act, good things generally happen—the music starts, the lights come up or go down, the games begin.

With a theatrical flourish, they're often the life of the party, clever and full of fun. Even routine activities can be made exciting.

New experiences and challenges are constantly sought. Promoter apes are bold and daring, ever optimistic and confident that everything will work out in the end. They thrive on risk and seem exhilarated in the face of danger.

These individuals excel under pressure, and are skilled at negotiating during tense situations and deal-making. You want a promoter ape around when a hero is needed or required.

Promoter apes typically prefer the finer amenities of life—pricy dining, expensive toys, luxurious entertainment, and high-end fashion.

They are often seen by others as sophisticated and seem to know everybody. They *are* the definition of "working the room."

Charming and confident, promoter apes have an endless supply of amazing stories and hilarious jokes, shared with ease and flair. They live in the moment and thrive on the unexpected.

Likewise, they become quickly bored with routine and stability, preferring instead to mix things up.

Performer Apes (ESFP – 11 percent)

These individuals live to entertain. Their warmth, good humor, and extraordinary skills in music, comedy, and drama make them fun to be around and elevate them to serving as the life of any good party. Their motivation seems to be to stimulate a positive response from their audience—no matter how large or small.

Performer apes are particularly uncomfortable being alone. They seek out company of any kind whenever and wherever possible.

Smooth, talkative, and witty, they are always ready to share the latest stories, jokes, wisecracks, and wordplay—nothing is too serious or sacred to escape being the subject of a good story or joke.

They enjoy living at light speed, complete with the latest fashions, food, drink, and music. Pleasure-seeking is an end unto itself, and performer apes will try most anything that promises excitement and good times.

Performer apes tend to look at the bright side and may have a tendency to ignore negative consequences, perhaps hoping they will resolve on their own.

Crafter/Warrior Apes (ISTP – 6 percent)

As the first of two introverted ape temperaments, crafter/warrior apes easily master the operation of tools, equipment, technologies, and instruments of all types. Even at a young age, these individuals naturally pick up tools and intuitively know how to use them, quickly becoming adept and skilled.

Their "toys" may include fast and powerful cars, motorcycles, boats, hunting and fishing gear, scuba gear, and more.

These are to be enjoyed to the fullest when the spontaneous mood hits. Actually, even the tools are more to be played with than used for work.

Like other apes, crafter/warriors take pleasure in plying their skills in dangerous and high-risk situations, which can potentially lead to injury. As introverts, they are more doers than talkers, which can make it challenging for others to get to know them.

While they can be fun and supportive with projects they find fascinating, they can quickly become insubordinate when bored or forced to do something against their will, rejecting authority and rules that are confining or limiting. Above all, they value freedom.

Composer Apes (ISFP – 6 percent)

Individuals of this temperament are fully in tune with their environments, especially when it comes to color, tone, texture, aroma, and flavor. They instinctively sense what belongs and what does not, as well as what is artistically pleasing and what is not.

They have the ability to fully immerse themselves in their artistic efforts, which can result in the spectacular. They often choose music, drawing, painting, sculpting, dance, or other art forms for self-expression.

Socially, they are unmatched in their kindness and generosity, and are particularly sensitive and sympathetic to the pain and suffering of others.

Composer apes are more likely to put in long, arduous hours pursuing their art, which can be misinterpreted by other temperaments as being antisocial. Not as attuned to or interested in verbal communication, they are highly skilled in the nonverbal, relying on their senses to experience life.

Some composer apes have natural connections with animals. They are sometimes described by others as animal whisperers.

The Dolphins (NFs – 14 percent)

The dolphin temperaments share an intense desire to know others and be known themselves, as well as attain personal potential and help others to do the same. They share intuition (N) and feeling (F). Their intuitive side relies on impressions and creativity, focusing on the big picture and looking for patterns and meaning. Their feeling side causes them to reserve judgement of others in favor of forgiveness, empathy, and warmth.

They differ in extroversion (E) vs. introversion (I) and judging (J) vs. perceiving (P).

The four dolphins include Teachers (ENFJ), Champions (ENFP), Counselors (INFJ), and Healers (INFP).

Teacher Dolphins (ENFJ – 4 percent)

Individuals with this temperament have a driving desire to lead others to reach for personal potential.

Teacher dolphins dream up an endless supply of activities and examples to fascinate and engage the imagination. Each human being, they believe, possesses untold potential that must be discovered and developed. Each individual could be the next Mozart or Einstein.

No matter what professions they choose, teacher dolphins consider people to be their highest priority, and they are willing to become personally involved. Warm and outgoing, they naturally exude concern.

They tend to be articulate and communicate face to

face especially well, not hesitant to share their feelings and ideas.

Overflowing with enthusiasm, teacher dolphins speak passionately and with flourish, showing charisma as public speakers. They prefer to be settled and organized, planning far in advance. They are trustworthy, faithfully meeting their obligations.

Teacher dolphins tend to be popular in their professional and social circles. They seem able to establish rapport with anyone, in part because they are highly tolerant, non-judgmental, and supportive.

Champion Dolphins (ENFP – 7 percent)

As the most prevalent dolphin, champion dolphins consider intense emotions to be necessary and vital to their lives.

They display a wide range of emotions, as well as a passion for the innovative. Life is exciting, full of possibilities—both positive and negative (though they don't dwell on the latter).

Described by others as bubbly, they often find it enjoyable to share their extraordinary experiences with others, talking tirelessly. Their excitement can be contagious and serve as a way for them to inspire others to try what they've described, based solely upon their recommendations. They are clearly the most vivacious of all the temperaments, often bordering on dramatic.

Champion dolphins are quick to pick up on environmental subtleties, scanning the room and sensing the general mood, as well as that of individuals. Not much escapes their attention.

They are talented at relationship-building, and typically have a large number and wide range of friends. They are seen by others as both likable and authentic, publicly shining with warmth and energy, and giving off positive and affirming vibes.

Counselor Dolphins (INFJ – 1 percent)

It is exceedingly rare to find a counselor dolphin. These individuals are strongly concerned for the welfare of others, receiving fulfillment by quietly contributing to and interacting with them. Counselor dolphins are nurturers, guiding others to meet personal potential.

While they are adept in social settings, they prefer solitude, especially when working on intensive tasks that require attention to detail.

Counselor dolphins are especially bothered by superficial interactions and relationships.

As introverts, they are not typically found up front leading out. Instead, they prefer to work behind the scenes, one-to-one or by themselves.

Since they are careful to keep their innermost thoughts and emotions to themselves, they can prove difficult to get to know—except when sharing with trusted individuals who are close to them.

Once others break through, they will find a rich, complicated inner world with powerful emotions. Friends and colleagues may be surprised, even after many years, to find new sides to counselor dolphins.

Their value for harmony helps counselor dolphins work well in organizations. They are attuned to subtle patterns of interactions in various groups, quickly recognizing the emotions and intentions of others—sometimes before those individuals themselves are aware.

With a vivid imagination, counselor dolphins often speak and write with poetic imagery even in their everyday communication. They are especially articulate in face-to-face meetings.

Among the various temperaments, counselor dolphins are more likely to believe they are somewhat clairvoyant, sensing impending danger or good fortune.

Healer Dolphins (INFP – 2 percent)

Even though healer dolphins may come across as calm and serene—even shy or distant—to those around them they have a deep capacity for caring.

They prefer a few quality friends with whom they share deep connections, and they usually support a favorite cause or passion.

Healer dolphins typically possess a strong desire to solve conflicts that divide others, bringing healing to their loved ones, friends, colleagues, community, and the world at large.

To healer dolphins, the world is an ethical, honorable place, brimming with possibilities and potential good. They possess a strong sense of right and wrong, but they typically keep their feelings and beliefs to themselves, which can lead to isolation.

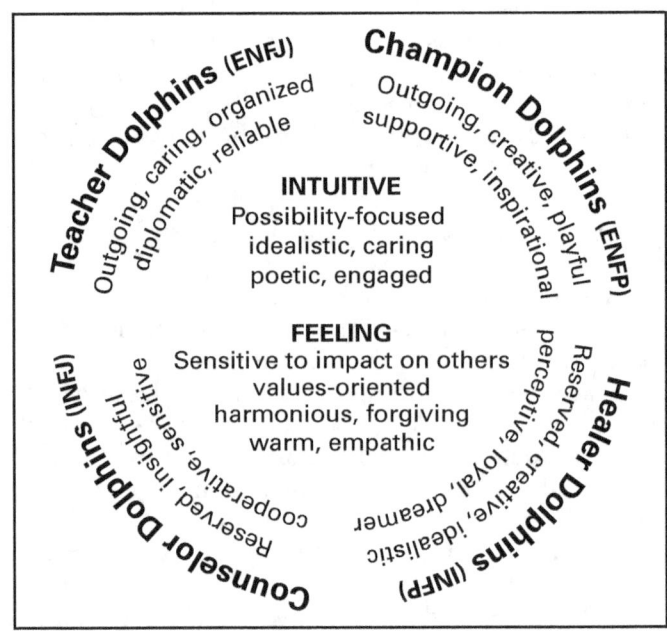

They are strongly committed and positive, often willing to sacrifice their own happiness for the good of others.

As children, healer dolphins are sometimes perceived as living in a world of fantasy and unrealistic idealism. They may be described by others as "having their head in the clouds." Sadly, they may come to view these tendencies as undesirable when parents, siblings, friends, and authority figures belittle them. They sometimes see themselves as the baby swan—the ugly duckling—surrounded by ordinary ducks.

At work, healer dolphins are adaptable and likable, welcoming new ideas and information. They show great patience with complicated scenarios, as well as impatience with routine. They are quite content—and probably prefer—to work by themselves. They follow their hearts and are intimately in touch with their feelings.

Healer dolphins are often drawn to scholarly pursuits, and are adept at creating and telling stories.

The Owls (NTs – 12 percent)

Owls are rarest among the four temperament families overall, sharing intuition (N) and thinking (T). Their intuition values creativity and focuses on the big picture, concepts, and interpretation. Their judging side prefers no surprises, with careful planning and preparation, and preferring to have matters settled.

They vary in extroversion (E) vs. introversion (I), and judging (J) vs. perceiving (P), representing intellectuals. The owls include Fieldmarshals (ENTJ), Inventors (ENTP), Masterminds (INTJ), and Architects (INTP).

Fieldmarshal Owls (ENTJ – 4 percent)

Competing with supervisor bears for leadership roles, fieldmarshal owls seek out leadership, but for very different reasons. Supervisor bears are more interested in logistical planning and preserving the corporate structure, while fieldmarshal owls focus on overarching policies and long-term goals, as well as strategizing how to reach or exceed them.

Fieldmarshal owls instinctively build organizations and implement goals—whether in the military, business, education, or government. They can clearly see where an organization should head and are able to communicate that vision to colleagues.

They also excel at systematizing, prioritizing, generalizing, summarizing, assembling evidence, and demonstrating their ideas. However, they will likely ask inventor or architect owls to actually examine the evidence for them and report back.

Fieldmarshal owls relish being in charge—a desire they've likely had since childhood, where they naturally assumed leadership roles. They tend to be tireless to a fault in their efforts, which can lead to an imbalance.

Short- and long-range objectives must be constantly revisited, and every action should be goal-driven, free of emotions and feelings. Decisions are based upon impersonal data and result in thoughtful, well-engineered plans and actions.

As leaders, fieldmarshal owls are intent on reducing red tape, redundancy, and confusion in the workplace. They are willing to dismiss employees who prove to be incompetent or who represent redundancy.

Ineffective people and procedures are quickly abandoned when they fail to support goals and meet expectations.

Inventor Owls (ENTP – 5 percent)

Representing the largest owl temperament, inventor owls are obsessed with building and fixing gadgets and machines. Their obsession is often first displayed in early childhood and continues for their entire lives. With help from others, they are able to turn their inventions into both social and manufacturing enterprises.

Their entrepreneurial natures drive inventor owls to continually look for ways "to invent a better mousetrap." When they hear the words, "This is the way we've always done it," that alone is reason enough for them to launch into finding a new and better way.

Inventor owls are intensely curious, forever asking how and why. They value ideas that naturally lead to action and are fascinated by complexity.

Prototypes are a means to an end—whether the end represents a new product in the marketplace or simply a better way to operate. They are practical, trusting their own skills and ideas. Needless to say, following a blueprint is against their very nature; they prefer to let their vision of the end product drive the process.

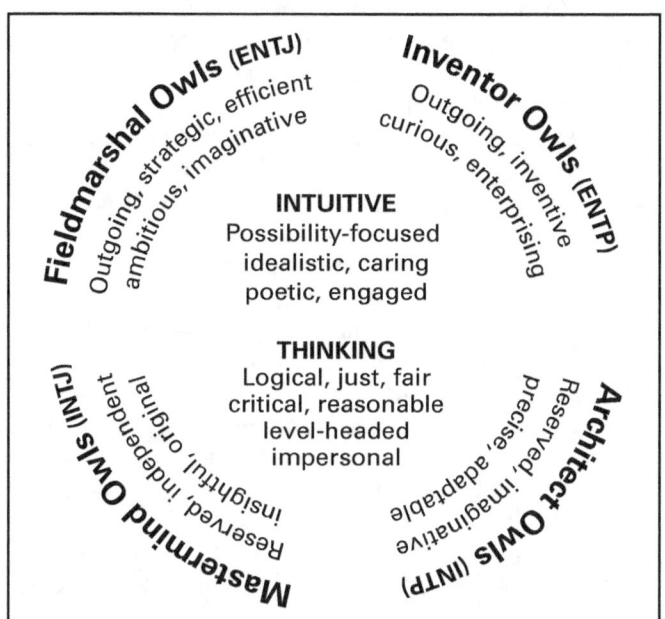

Inventor owls typically enjoy notoriety among their "groupie" friends who enthusiastically listen to and challenge their ideas—in a friendly, supportive way of course. They tend to be easygoing, seldom taking the time or having the interest to criticize others. They are skilled conversationalists.

Inventor owls do not flourish in humdrum jobs or activities with predictable routines and outcomes. They are particularly useful on teams involved with developing pilot projects and creating prototypes.

Inventor owls are sensitive to the politics of organizations, seeking to understand people as they relate to systems and strategies.

They are adept at rising to the challenge, especially when they're told, "It can't be done." Their instinctive response is to say, "Stand back and watch me succeed."

Mastermind Owls (INTJ – 1 percent)

These individuals have the distinction of sharing the smallest temperament position with counselor dolphins. While mastermind owls are good at operational planning, they excel at mentally exploring every contingency. They are able to understand and develop complex steps, with one naturally leading to the next.

When they encounter a step that is ineffective, they instinctively consider alternatives and mentally follow the likely results of each action.

Efficiency is indispensable in any operation, and any waste of human or material resources calls for immediate realignment or reassignment.

Rules and procedures are non-binding, and neither traditional authority nor technical jargon impress them. Only sensible ideas are worth considering. Competency is a priority, both for themselves and for associates. *And no one should ever make the same mistake twice.*

Mastermind owls are especially energized by tangled systems and problems that require careful and creative sorting. Their pragmatic and practical approach calls for patience and thoroughness.

They tend to be positive in their suggestions and criticisms, but can become hard-nosed if progress is too slow or not forthcoming.

Of all the owls, masterminds display the most decisiveness and self-confidence, as well as a strong will. They are driven to make decisions, then commit even when the unexpected happens. They insist on knowing the facts before making decisions, and are particularly suspicious of ideas that are based on questionable or untested data.

Architect Owls (INTP – 2 percent)

The 16th temperament comprises the architect owl, master designer. From blueprints to theoretical systems, from school curricula to corporate strategies, the world

Supervisor Bears 13%
Provider Bears 12%
Performer Apes 11%
Promoter Apes 10%
Inspector Bears 9%
Protector Bears 7%
Champion Dolphins 7%
Crafter/Warrior Apes 6%
Composer Apes 6%
Inventor Owls 5%
Teacher Dolphins 4%
Fieldmarshal Owls 4%
Healer Dolphins 2%
Architect Owls 2%
Counselor Dolphins 1%
Mastermind Owls 1%

exists to be scrutinized, explained, then fixed or redesigned. The only purpose of the external world, with its physical raw materials, is to organize and restructure it.

Architect owls are fascinated by natural principles and laws. They are able to effortlessly recognize distinctions and inconsistencies. Their designs are elegant, efficient, and coherent.

They are precise communicators, both publicly and interpersonally, and cannot help themselves but point out the errors they observe. They have little time for idle chit chat.

Position and celebrity have no value. Even someone with an average IQ may spark an idea in their minds that could lead to pure genius. They will listen to anybody, regardless of prestige, rank, or social status in their search for answers.

Architect owls may seem somewhat shy and distant except with close friends. They prefer to work alone and in the quiet, sitting in front of a computer screen or drafting table.

They tend to develop tunnel vision when deep into a project, problem, or idea, and they will persevere until they feel they understand and can solve a problem.

Temperament and Parenting

The nuclear family is the first place that we, as human beings, begin to relate to others. The traditional family system, beginning when Adam and Eve were joined by their first children, Cain and Abel, comprises a parental team and offspring. How they relate to each other on the various levels provides the foundation for all future relationships for children.

The importance of the family system cannot be overstated. Leading the family system is a parental team—traditionally a husband and wife. The strength of the parental team is key to establishing parent-child relationships as well as sibling to sibling.

Our first relationship takes place *in utero*. Much about this initial connection with our mothers impacts the rest of our lives. One by one, key individuals enter our environment—fathers, siblings, relatives, family friends, acquaintances, peers, authority figures, colleagues, bosses, and a faceless sea of people with whom we cross paths and interact throughout our lives.

We don't choose our families—anymore than we choose our physical characteristics or temperament. In other relationships, we can decide with whom we will spend our time and avoid those we dislike. With our families, we're stuck with our parents and siblings. Nothing we do will change to whom we were born and with whom we share our parents.

The Parental Team

In the past three to four decades, marriage counselors have utilized temperament theory to address issues of compatibility for couples.

In the mid-1980s, when my then-fiancé and I were moving toward marriage, we attended a pre-marriage seminar, designed to help us discover and strengthen various aspects of our romantic relationship.

The seminar leaders—the dean of my dormitory and his wife—included the MBTI as part of our experience. In a face-to-face counseling session with this couple, we were told that we were compatible *and nothing more.*

What did that mean, who decided we were compatible, and what was their process?

In most circles, temperament theory continues to be a mysterious tool utilized by professionals and rarely explained in any detail to laypeople.

Our pre-marital experience was considered to be quite advanced and innovative. When our parents were entering the romantic periods of their lives, the culture in the United States was in the process of moving from arranged marriages to personal choice.

At that point, compatibility wasn't even part of the conversation. As long as your spouse was of the opposite sex (and breathing), practiced the same religion, was part of a similar social class, and came from a family of appropriate political beliefs, you were a match.

But the marital team becomes the parental team. Temperament compatibility is a critical part of creating a strong parental team.

In the illustration below, the first track is typical of the vast majority of marital relationships, leading to a growing number of divorces. A minority of marriages survive in their original state.

Temperament theory offers an alternative track. In order to create a strong parental team, the marriage must first be repaired and bonds strengthened.

continued on page 26

Attraction → Conflict → Contempt → Rejection

Attraction	Conflict	Contempt	Rejection
Alike, mystery envy	Familiarity, deficits	Stupid, wrong, bad, won't change	Leave, ignore, give up

Two approaches; different outcomes

Conflict → Tolerate → Appreciate → Value

Conflict	Tolerate	Appreciate	Value
Characteristics are stupid, bad, wrong	Born with characteristics	Differences are good	Differences are helpful and useful

Monitors STJ
Caretakers of
organizations,
objects, information

Extrovert:
Supervisor Bear
ESTJ

Introvert:
Inspector Bear
ISTJ

**Bears SJs
Guardians**

*Take Care
of the World*

Conservators SFJ
Caretakers of
people's
physical needs

Extrovert:
Provider Bear
ESFJ

Introvert:
Protector Bear
ISFJ

CONCRETE
Sensing, tangible

*Use/enjoy
the World*

Operators STP
Outdo and
overtake

Extrovert:
Promoter Ape
ESTP

Introvert:
Crafter/Warrior Ape
ISTP

**Apes SPs
Artisans**

Players SFP
Excite and please
self and others

Extrovert:
Performer Ape
ESFP

Introvert:
Composer Ape
ISFP

Extrovert:
Teacher Dolphin
ENFJ

Introvert:
Counselor Dolphin
INFJ

Mentors NFJ
Proactive facilitators
of human potential

**Dolphins NFs
Idealists**
*Seek
relationships*

Extrovert:
Champion Dolphin
ENFP

Introvert:
Healer Dolphin
INFP

Advocates NFP
Reactive facilitators
of human potenial

ABSTRACT
Intuition, unseen world

Extrovert:
Fieldmarshal Owl
ENTJ

Introvert:
Mastermind Owl
INTJ

Organizers NTJ
Bring order
to chaos

*Seek
knowledge*
**Owls NTs
Intellectuals**

Extrovert:
Inventor Owl
ENTP

Introvert:
Architect Owl
INTP

Engineers NTP
Ingenuity and
innovation

continued from page 23
Establishing a strong parental team begins with moving from temperament-based conflict to compromise and consensus.

Contempt. Because people truly believe they have the power to change others—through force, discipline, manipulation, or by other more sinister means—their feelings toward their marital partner often lead to contempt and disappointment once they fail to "persuade" their partner to change. This is usually followed by rejection in the form of estrangement and divorce.

These individuals are oblivious to the fact that human beings are fundamentally different from each other, and those differences are genetically driven. They see others with different beliefs and behaviors as threatening, wrong, bad, or downright stupid. They deride the perceived "deficits" they see in others.

This is the basis for virtually all world conflicts, from country against country to "me versus you." The inability or refusal to accept differences in others is fundamental to the process of conflict.

Temperament theory seeks to turn this process upside down, reversing the downward spiral typical of many human relationships.

Conflict. Most conflict is rooted in misunderstanding and resulting distrust. The natural antidote is—well—understanding. By sharing knowledge about the inherent differences in human beings that are fundamentally unchangeable, people are able to move to the next steps, which are …

Tolerance. Once human beings are able to recognize the fundamental differences between themselves and others, and that people are born with differing characteristics already in place, they usually find it easier to tolerate others.

Our world is marked by intolerance, rooted in identity theory—the most destructive and divisive approach to human interaction that exists.

The differences between races and genders pale in relation to temperament differences. The four basic temperament families, each with their four specific temperaments, are present in every race, culture, and society on the planet. People should never be prejudged as a group because of skin color, gender, or any other characteristic with which they were born and over which they have zero choice.

Appreciation. Once human beings learn to tolerate the genetically based temperaments with which they and others around them were born, the next step is to begin appreciating these characteristics within themselves and in others.

Our Creator values diversity and uniqueness. Just as there are no two identical snowflakes, there are no two identical human beings. Identical twins will show marked differences, even when they are reared in the same environment. Clones, identical to an even greater extent, will grow up to be different.

That's a good thing! Imagine a football team with all quarterbacks or defensive linemen. That team would be non-functional and easily defeated.

Human "teams" of every kind need the skills and perspectives that the various temperaments bring in order to be successful in any shared endeavor.

Value. The final step is to learn to value the differences—not just appreciate them. For married couples, that means identifying the strengths of their partner, valuing them, and relying on those strengths to benefit the team. It also means accepting the flaws.

Parents are given the task of training their children to become useful participants in society. For those parents who are very similar in temperament to their offspring, the process of raising their children may seem far easier and more successful to observers. Indeed, they have far less "work" to do in shaping their children, as well as loving and supporting them.

Similar to the process of learning to appreciate and value each other, parents would do well to begin by accepting their children "as is." Attempting to change temperament characteristics in their children can be compared to paddling upstream on a river. The greater the temperament differences between parent and child, the faster the current on this proverbial river.

Paddling upstream will eventually wear them down. Why not work with a child's temperament, rather than attempting to change it through coercion, punishment, and contempt? Many children have spent years in therapy dealing with low self-esteem and self-loathing *resulting from parental disapproval.*

Temperament Matches

Within the family system, there are two major benefits to learning and applying temperament theory. First, parents will learn to understand, tolerate, appreciate, and value each other. Second, they will apply the same process to their children.

As a review, the Myers-Briggs continua suggest that everyone falls somewhere on each continuum:

- **Extroversion** (E) ⟷ **Introversion** (I)
- **Sensing** (S) ⟷ **Intuition** (N)
- **Thinking** (T) ⟷ **Feeling** (F)
- **Judging** (J) ⟷ **Perceiving** (P)

Keep in mind that very few people will land at either pole; the vast majority are positioned somewhere between the poles. The closer we are to the center of each continuum, the more challenging it will be to decide on which side we belong.

Some of that confusion is caused by authority figures or peers who have tried to steer us to be more like them—as if they are right and we are wrong.

However, the process of attempting to determine our positions on the four continua is worth the effort.

Our four-letter MBTI codes are matched to the animal families—bears, apes, dolphins, and owls—suggested by Keith Golay, with the goal of making temperament theory interesting and memorable, rather than simply SJs, SPs, NFs, and NTs.

Logically, the more similar the temperaments of the parental team, the more intrinsic agreement will occur. The more dissimilar the temperaments, the greater the dissonance on virtually every decision and the greater the need for loving discussion.

Yet, in order for the parental team to function as an impenetrable, united front, compromise and consensus must be reached *on every issue* involving the children. A divided parental team will lead to discrepancies in parenting styles. On the surface, many intelligent children will seek to divide and conquer the parental team, but deep down—whether they realize it or not—they want their parents to remain strong and resist their challenges to parental authority.

Dissonance and conflict within the family system *will result* from the following scenarios:
- One parent dominates—not just leads—the team and makes all of the rules, shutting out and demeaning the other parent.
- Fundamental differences in temperament will lead to conflicting parental motivations and values.
- Temperament differences are labeled right or wrong, defined by a dominant parent.
- Parents of similar temperament have two children—one of similar temperament and the other vastly different, setting up a "black sheep" and favored child scenario.
- Parents of different temperaments side with the child that is nearer their temperament, setting up unhealthy alliances and alignments.

Rules for Healthy Parenting
- Set up your parental rules and guidelines during quiet, calm moments away from the children.
- Decide ahead of time how you will handle a child who is trying to divide and conquer the parental team—which will almost certainly take place.
- Be willing to compromise—but always in private.

Opposite Temperaments
(nothing in common; a recipe for conflict and misunderstanding)

ESTJ Supervisor Bear	≠	**INFP** Healer Dolphin
ISTJ Inspector Bear	≠	**ENFP** Champion Dolphin
ESFJ Providor Bear	≠	**INTP** Architect Owl
ISFJ Protector Bear	≠	**ENTP** Inventor Owl
ESTP Promoter Ape	≠	**INFJ** Counselor Dolphin
ISTP Crafter/Warrior Ape	≠	**ENFJ** Teacher Dolphin
ESFP Performer Ape	≠	**INTJ** Mastermind Owl
ISFP Composer Ape	≠	**ENTJ** Fieldmarshal Owl

• Never interfere while one parent is disciplining a child—except for potential physical, verbal, or emotional abuse. Avoid embarrassing the other parent in front of the children *at all costs*.

• Do not make major parenting decisions without consulting each other (inform your children that Mom and Dad need to talk first).

• Identify the temperament of each child and jointly create unique strategies for guiding and disciplining.

• Never punish a child when angry; postpone it until calm has fully returned for everyone.

• Use self-soothing as a reason to step away and cool down—both for parents and children.

• Agree that nothing about your child is inherently wrong, bad, or evil (repeat until you believe it).

• First, strive to be the best spouse you can be; second, strive to be the best parent you can be.

Two archetypal parenting styles are worth mentioning both for awareness and avoidance.

Raging Father. This archetype is described as a dominant father who uses intimidation, shaming, and guilting to beat down his spouse as well as his children. He rules with an iron fist, severely punishing anyone who steps out of line.

Devouring Mother. This archetype is described as a dominant mother who keeps at bay the raging father (or any father), protecting children from perceived abuse (i.e., discipline, responsibility, consequences, etc.) and preserving their immaturity and dependence on her.

Both of these archetypes are far more common than you may believe—particularly the devouring mother, whose parenting leads to non-resilient children who "wilt" easily under the reality of life.

The current culture in the United States has increasingly become feminized, with masculine characteristics publicly shamed. As a result, young men in particular are emotionally destroyed, feeling powerless and helpless. *Could this be a reason for violent reactions?*

Resolving Conflict
In following chapters, the limbic system will be

Matching One Characteristic

Individuals who share only one characteristic will be spending a great deal of time in the world of the other (parental partner or child).

With little in common, there needs to be increased sensitivity to temperament differences and a willingness to allow the other to recharge as needed—*without judgement.*

Extroverted (outgoing)	*Sensing* (physical)	*Thinking* (logical)	*Judging* (decisive)
ESTJ Supervisor Bear	**ESTJ** Supervisor Bear	**ESTJ** Supervisor Bear	**ESTJ** Supervisor Bear
ENFP Champion Dolphin	**ISFP** Composer Ape	**INTP** Architect Owl	**INFJ** Counselor Dolphin
ESFJ Provider Bear	**ESFJ** Provider Bear	**ESTP** Promoter Ape	**ESFJ** Provider Bear
ENTP Inventor Owl	**ISTP** Crafter/Warrior Ape	**INTJ** Mastermind Owl	**INTJ** Mastermind Owl
ESTP Promoter Ape	**ESTP** Promoter Ape	**ENTP** Inventor Owl	**ENFJ** Teacher Dolphin
ENFJ Teacher Dolphin	**ISFJ** Protector Bear	**ISTJ** Inspector Bear	**ISTJ** Inspector Bear
ESFP Performer Ape	**ESFP** Performer Ape	**ENTJ** Fieldmarshal Owl	**ENTJ** Fieldmarshal Owl
ENTJ Fieldmarshal Owl	**ISTJ** Inspector Bear	**ISTP** Crafter/Warrior Ape	**ISFJ** Protector Bear

Introverted (reserved)	*Intuitive* (impression)	*Feeling* (people-focused)	*Perceiving* (open-ended)
ISTJ Inspector Bear	**ENFP** Champion Dolphin	**ESFP** Performer Ape	**ESTP** Promoter Ape
INFP Healer Dolphin	**INTJ** Mastermind Owl	**INFJ** Counselor Dolphin	**INFP** Healer Dolphin
ISFJ Protector Bear	**ENTP** Inventor Owl	**ESFJ** Protector Bear	**ESFP** Performer Ape
INTP Architect Owl	**INFJ** Counselor Dolphin	**INFP** Healer Dolphin	**INTP** Architect Owl
ISTP Crafter/Warrior Owl	**ENFJ** Teacher Dolphin	**ENFP** Champion Dolphin	**ENFP** Champion Dolphin
INFJ Counselor Dolphin	**INTP** Architect Owl	**ISFJ** Protector Bear	**ISTP** Crafter/Warrior Ape
ISFP Composer Ape	**ENTJ** Fieldmarshal Owl	**ENFJ** Teacher Dolphin	**ENTP** Inventor Owl
INTJ Mastermind Owl	**INFP** Healer Dolphin	**ISFP** Composer Ape	**ISFP** Composer Ape

discussed, as well as ways to calm limbic responses and remain in control.

However, a basic understanding of the various temperaments evident in one's family circle will help explain many of the conflicts and issues that arise within a family system, as well as provide ideas for solutions and resolutions.

Two or Three Shared Temperament Traits

Shared temperament traits with someone does not guarantee relational success, since there are so many experiential factors that cause attraction or animosity.

However, those with two or three common traits are more likely to resonate with thought processes and rationales, leading to mutual values and perspectives. Relationships are built upon shared experiences and ideas, and common traits between two individuals increase the likelihood they will agree with each other's ideas and conclusions.

There are exceptions to every rule. Two temper-

aments who probably shouldn't attempt a long-term relationship are Supervisor Bears (ESTJ) and Fieldmarshal Owls (ENTJ). They vary by one letter, but both temperaments are instinctive leaders and unlikely to yield to the other. In addition, their leadership styles and motivations for leading are entirely different.

Trying to Live in the World of Another for Too Long

Family systems will require various members to step into the worlds of the others on a regular basis. The parental team—the most intimate of all human relationships—requires the greatest amount of time in the world of the other when temperaments do not match.

It's relatively easy to exist in the world of someone who is very similar. When both relational partners are energized by the same events and activities, as well as rested and recharged in the same ways, there is little need for understanding and accommodation.

The greater the differences, the more effort will be needed, and permission must be freely given for each

---

Matching Two or Three Characteristics *(best)*

Extroverted/Sensing	*Introverted/Sensing*	*Sensing/Thinking*	*Intuitive/Thinking*
ESTJ Supervisor Bear	**ISTJ** Inspector Bear	**ESTJ** Supervisor Bear	**ENTJ** Fieldmarshal Owl
ESTP Promoter Ape	**ISTP** Crafter/Warrior Ape	**ISTP** Crafter/Warrior Ape	**INTJ** Mastermind Owl
ESFP Performer Ape	**ISFP** Composer Ape	**ESTP** Promoter Ape	**ENTP** Inventor Owl
ESFJ Provider Bear	**ISFJ** Protector Bear	**ISTJ** Inspector Bear	**INTP** Architect Owl
Extroverted/Intuitive	*Introverted/Intuitive*	*Sensing/Feeling*	*Intuitive/Feeling*
ENTJ Fieldmarshal Owl	**INTJ** Mastermind Owl	**ESFJ** Provider Bear	**ENFJ** Teacher Dolphin
ENTP Inventor Owl	**INTP** Architect Owl	**ISFP** Composer Ape	**INFJ** Counselor Dolphin
ENFP Champion Dolphin	**INFP** Healer Dolphin	**ESFP** Performer Ape	**ENFP** Champion Dolphin
ENFJ Teacher Dolphin	**INFJ** Counselor Dolphin	**ISFJ** Protector Bear	**INFP** Healer Dolphin
Extroverted/Thinking	*Introverted/Thinking*	*Sensing/Judging*	*Intuitive/Judging*
ESTJ Supervisor Bear	**ISTJ** Inspector Bear	**ESFJ** Provider Bear	**ENFJ** Teacher Dolphin
ESTP Promoter Ape	**ISTP** Crafter/Warrior Ape	**ISTJ** Inspector Bear	**INFJ** Counselor Dolphin
ENTP Inventor Owl	**INTP** Architect Owl	**ESTJ** Supervisor Bear	**ENTJ** Fieldmarshal Owl
ENTJ Fieldmarshal Owl	**INTJ** Mastermind Owl	**ISFJ** Protector Bear	**INTJ** Mastermind Owl
Extroverted/Feeling	*Introverted/Feeling*	*Sensing/Perceiving*	*Intuitive/Perceiving*
ESFJ Provider Bear	**ISFJ** Protector Bear	**ESTP** Promoter Ape	**ENTP** Inventor Owl
ESFP Performer Ape	**ISFP** Composer Ape	**ISTP** Crafter/Warrior Ape	**INTP** Architect Owl
ENFP Champion Dolphin	**INFP** Healer Dolphin	**ESFP** Performer Ape	**ENFP** Champion Dolphin
ENFJ Teacher Dolphin	**INFJ** Counselor Dolphin	**ISFP** Composer Ape	**INFP** Healer Dolphin
Extroverted/Judging	*Introverted/Judging*	*Thinking/Judging*	*Feeling/Judging*
ENTJ Fieldmarshal Owl	**ISTJ** Inspector Bear	**ESTJ** Supervisor Bear	**ESFJ** Provider Bear
ENFJ Teacher Dolphin	**ISFJ** Protector Bear	**ISTJ** Inspector Bear	**ISFJ** Protector Bear
ESFJ Provider Bear	**INFJ** Counselor Dolphin	**ENTJ** Fieldmarshal Owl	**ENFJ** Teacher Dolphin
ESTJ Supervisor Bear	**INTJ** Mastermind Owl	**INTJ** Mastermind Owl	**INFJ** Counselor Dolphin
Extroverted/Perceiving	*Introverted/Perceiving*	*Thinking/Perceiving*	*Feeling/Perceiving*
ENTP Inventor Owl	**ISTP** Crafter/Warrior Ape	**ESTP** Promoter Ape	**ESFP** Performer Ape
ENFP Champion Dolphin	**ISFP** Composer Ape	**ISTP** Crafter/warrior Ape	**ISFP** Composer Ape
ESFP Performer Ape	**INFP** Healer Dolphin	**ENTP** Champion Dolphin	**ENFP** Champion Dolphin
ESTP Promoter Ape	**INTP** Architect Owl	**INTP** Healer Dolphin	**INFP** Healer Dolphin

partner to routinely return to his or her own world to recharge. This principle applies to all family relationships—from the parental team to parent-child as well as sibling-to-sibling.

Learning Styles

Teachers will tell you that students in a classroom learn in entirely different and contrasting ways. The challenge is to integrate a variety of teaching techniques into the classroom to not only meet scholastic needs but motivate each student to engage and achieve.

Following are some learning styles suggested in a presentation titled "The Four Types and Learning Types in Children: Based on the Myers-Briggs Type Indicator," given by J. Patrick Howley.[1]

These principles are valuable for anyone interested in temperament theory and understanding what drives human behavior.

Bears (sensing + judging, SJ)

Overarching goal: to serve and be responsible.
- Hungers for belonging.
- Likes to make decisions.
- Wants to please authority figures.

_____

[1] https://slideplayer.com/slide/12312378/

Living in the World of the Other …

In any healthy relationship, it's important for both partners to be willing to step into the world of the other, as well as be sensitive when it's been enough.

Extrovert vs. Introvert

Extroverts love parties and gatherings. They work the room and are energized by interacting with others. If the partner is an an introvert, the extrovert will need to look for signs—implicit or explicit—that the introvert has had enough. Introverts will enjoy more intimate settings with fewer people—or being alone. A sensitive extrovert is willing to participate in more intimate activities, such as a quiet meal or walk on the beach, or even allow the introvert to be alone *without judgment.* There is give and take, with each partner stepping into the world of the other as an act of love, caring, and compromise.

Sensing vs. Intuition

In a "discussion," sensing individuals will want tangible proof and examples, while intuitive individuals rely on impressions and patterns. This discrepancy can create an impasse. Each must learn to value the strengths of the other— one supplying the facts and the other noticing patterns and sharing impressions.

Thinking vs. Feeling

Thinking individuals will believe that others should suffer the consequences of their actions, while feeling individuals are more likely to protect others from consequences. Both perspectives temper each other and are valuable.

Judging vs. Perceiving

Judging individuals prefer to make decisions and stick to them, while perceiving individuals like options, spontaneity, and improvisation. Hmmm…

… But Stepping Back to Recharge

- Prefers and needs structure and pre-planning.
- Needs predictability
- Change and unpredictability are unnerving.
- Works hard first, then plays later.
- Wants clear directions about tasks.
- Learns best with questions and answers.
- Does well responding to questions in writing.
- Easily conforms to standards set by authority.
- Prefers studying facts.
- Focuses on the present—*what actually is.*
- Has a good sense of timing (able to predict how long it will take to a complete task).
- Works at a steady pace.
- Thrives in a consistent and stable environment.
- Does not like to "wing it" by guessing, inventing, or speculating.
- Prefers to use skills already learned.
- Likes formalized instruction and orderly sequences.
- Creates a tangible product that organizes and summarizes what's been learned.
- Works on projects in small groups to help each other out and unleash greater productivity.
- Wants clear goals spelled out and sequential.
- Needs clear markers for finishing one task and moving on to the next.
- Motivated by milestones, completion points, and little ceremonies to honor success.
- Withers under scrutiny and criticism.

Apes (sensing + perceiving, SP)

Overarching goal: to be free and autonomous.
- Hungers for action.
- Cheerful; brings fun and laughter to the world.
- Enjoys the unplanned and the unexpected.
- Acts spontaneously.
- Focuses on the present.
- Adapts well to change.
- Enjoys freedom to move around.
- Learns better when there are opportunities to perform or get out into the field.
- Tends to mistrust vague ideas.
- Is likely to have a good recall of details.
- Rebels against close supervision.
- Learns best in an environment with variety and a constant change of pace.
- Becomes bored with too much deskwork.
- Routines become deadly.
- Needs physical involvement in learning through "hands-on" experiences.
- Prefers experience over what's read.
- Likes gadgets and objects to explore and play with.
- Finds verbal interaction and visual objects more interesting.
- Thrives on competition.

- Prefers step-by-step learning and precise directions.
- Likes using skills already learned.
- Wants to make work fun.
- May start too many projects at once and have difficulty finishing them, or completes them with last-minute flurry of activity.
- May complete tasks late as a result of poor planning or time management.
- Learns best when first taught a manual skill related to the lesson.
- Likes multi-sensory activities, allowing for touch, manipulating things, and moving around.
- Enjoys opportunities for hands-on activities.
- Concrete learning style.
- Likes facts and skills applicable to current lives.
- Prefers first-hand experience that provides practice in the skills and concepts learned.
- Needs to know relevance of what's learned.
- Enjoys small groups, where discussion is more comfortable.
- Likes to solve problems in unique ways.
- Works well against a deadline.
- Needs tasks to make sense.
- Likes genuine choices (i.e. negotiable agreements).
- Needs facts and examples to describe issues.
- Responds positively to criticism and direction.

Dolphins (intuitive + feeling, or NF)

Overarching goal: to relate to others and meet human potential.
- Hungers for a sense of self.
- Views the world from a personal perspective.
- Is concerned about relationships and harmony.
- Needs to communicate in a personal way.
- Is hypersensitive to conflict, hostility, sarcasm, ridicule, and criticism.
- Avoids confrontation.
- Seeks to be known and relate to others personally.
- Enjoys discussion and role-playing.
- Needs opportunities to be original.
- Craves variety and dislikes routines.
- Learning style can be sporadic and random.
- Has skills for understanding others.
- Needs feedback and praise about performance.
- Is motivated by personal notes from others.
- Enjoys reading and working alone.
- Works in bursts with slower, less-productive periods in between.
- Prefers cooperative learning versus competitive.
- Likes subject matter focusing on people.
- Enjoys pleasing others, even in seemingly unimportant matters.
- Connects best with authority figures who value a personal rapport.

- May skip over facts or get them wrong.
- Likes to help choose how and what is learned.
- Enjoys examining values.
- Likes tasks with a goal of helping people.
- Needs affirmation for creativity and uniqueness.
- Works well in small peer groups.
- Considers human issues to be important.
- Enjoys subject matter about people and decisions that impact them.
- Criticism and guidance should be warm and caring.

Owls (intuitive + thinking, or NT)
Overarching goal: to be logical and competent.
- Needs opportunities to demonstrate competence.
- Values individual achievement.
- Is intellectually curious.
- Is concerned with principle-based truth and justice.
- Needs to know criteria for evaluations by others.
- Wants to understand, explain, predict, and control.
- Prefers a global (big picture) approach.
- Creates mental models.
- Spontaneously analyzes flaws in ideas, things, or people.
- Likes to prove points logically.
- Prefers independent learning and is self-motivated.
- Learns best from logical didactic presentations.
- Enjoys opportunities for self-instruction.
- Likes to do follow-up reading.
- Likes opportunities to be inventive and original.
- Needs feedback regarding specific, objective achievements.
- Wants to understand reasons why events occur.
- Wants to get on with serious learning; may see play as a waste of time.
- Focuses on the future, imagining what could be.
- Enjoys learning new skills more than mastering familiar ones.
- Finds ideas more interesting than people.
- Enjoys talking to older people more than peers.
- Prefers an overview that explains the purpose for learning subject matter.
- Wants to be an equal partner in learning, asking challenging questions and linking knowledge to other fields.
- Likes chances to problem-solve on his/her own.
- Enjoys working on cutting-edge problems.
- Likes learning which requires self-initiative.
- Needs authority figures to be logically organized.
- Enjoys tasks that require imagination.
- Gives and takes criticism easily.

It's a Bear World After All
Whether you like it or not, you live in a bear world. By most estimates, more than 40 percent of the world's population are one of the four bear temperaments.

That means your chances of being a bear or being in a relationship with a bear are extremely high.

In light of that, the approximately 60 percent of the population who are not bears must learn to cope with bear rules, policies, protocols, and expectations. *Period.*

You can spend your life fighting bear society, where following the rules and fulfilling your duty are paramount, you can create workarounds that allow your temperament to be okay with a structured and confining world, or you can try to work outside the bear world in a more creative and open-minded setting.

Workarounds
It is pointless to try to force change upon others—especially a parental partner or child. Forced change will require coercion, and the changes *will not be* permanent. Many are confused about who they really are, shamed by authority figures or peers. You cannot permanently alter your temperament any easier than you can change the color of your skin.

The world is largely run by bears, and other temperaments will need to develop "workarounds" to survive and thrive within an environment they may find limiting, restrictive, and outdated.

Those unable to tame their temperaments in order to work in bear environments may want to create their own space where they can make a living outside the confines of corporate society or in a setting that attracts non-bears—such as creativity-based fields.

Most organizations are bear-oriented. They value and reward responsibility, loyalty, timeliness, protocols, rules, and a number of other core principles that are assumed by bears to be universal.

In response, freedom-seeking apes may struggle with following rules, policies, procedures, protocols, and traditions—particularly those with which they disagree or that seem to thwart progress.

Owls do not intrinsically recognize or respect authority or status *at all*, driving bears crazy.

Dolphins are bothered when rules and policies do not allow for workers to grow and achieve their personal and professional potential. Authority figures who bully those below are especially despicable.

It is fruitless to try and alter the characteristics with which your parental partner or child was born; you will have far greater success if you work on the one individual you can change: *yourself*. Since relational systems are impacted by each individual component, you can bring about change by improving yourself. The behaviors of your family system *will change* in response.

Reframing. One of the most powerful tools available to individuals is the ability to reframe—simply restate situations in a way that sheds new light and resonates with you or a family member's temperament. Many individuals reframe instinctively without knowing that reframing "is a thing."

For instance, freedom-seeking individuals in particular may fail to prioritize being on time. Those whose attention becomes highly focused in a situation may simply lose track of time. Others try to do "just one more thing" and make themselves late. Still others do not plan efficiently for travel time or other details.

Whatever the reason for their tardiness, these individuals will need find other motivators to help them be on time in bear settings.

For apes, being on time can be viewed as a skill—as important as their other skills. Since they also strive to be impressive, timeliness can be postured as a way to impress others (*so be impressed when they're on time*).

Dolphins are consumed by relationships, so timeliness can be reframed as a way to show love and care for others. Being late, on the other hand, will hurt the feelings of others, as well as show disrespect.

Competence is a major theme for owls. Suggesting that timeliness is a sign of competence will help motivate them to pay attention to the clock—even when they're consumed by gathering new knowledge.

Soothing. When individuals become highly reactive, they are likely to lose their ability to behave rationally. Certain temperaments are naturally more reactive, but life experiences for all temperaments can result in unhealthy reactivity.

Families can develop routines for self-soothing and other-soothing. Discrete and subtle signals can be established ahead of time so that each knows when to step away and cool down—*without embarrassment*.

Respect. Hierarchies are fundamental to bear society. Bears value status and expect obedience to authority. Apes and owls may struggle with authority figures, whom they may see as narrow-minded, non-creative, or even incompetent. Dolphins will likely show respect for authority because they value relationships, abhor conflict, and seek to please others.

Conscientiousness. Since bears value reliability, dependability, and quality, it goes to reason that all three will be necessary requirements in order to hold a typical job or position.

Bears may perceive creativity as disrespect for established policies and protocols. Thinking through a process or problem may be seen as daydreaming. They may wonder how other temperaments accomplish anything worthwhile.

Once again, apes will want to be conscientious as a way to impress others. Owls will strive to be conscientious as evidence of competency. And dolphins may need to be reminded that conscientiousness is an ideal way to build strong relationships and establish trust.

Social skills. The ability to socially interact with other people is essential to success in life. You or a family member may struggle with social situations. However, out of love for each other, the non-social family member must be willing to be exposed to potentially uncomfortable settings, while the social family members are sensitive and supportive of the need to be alone and recharge.

Extroverted individuals will have fewer problems with social skills because they intrinsically crave the company of others. However, a third of the population is introverted, and the tendency to withdraw is often viewed as a problem. The term "shy" has negative connotations, often viewed as a developmental problem.

However, there is nothing wrong with shyness. But workarounds can be learned in order to survive and develop a level of personal comfort in social settings.

Moodiness. Most bears prefer predictability. A person who becomes intensely emotional for no apparent reason is viewed as a problem—a "loose cannon."

Therefore, it is important to practice self-soothing and avoid falling into emotional reactivity. As you will see in the next few chapters, there is an inverse relationship between emotional reactivity and intelligence.

Enlightened Selfishness. Human beings instinctively want the best for themselves—often at the expense of others. Christians will tell you that selfishness is the essence of sin. However, wanting the best for yourself can be a useful motivator for you to behave in ways that will benefit everyone with whom you interact.

Enlightened selfishness is the process of asking yourself—*before* you do or say anything—"Is this in my best interest?" The enlightened part informs you that mistreating others for selfish gain will create enemies, which is not in your personal best interest.

It is ultimately in your best interest to adapt to the environment in which you find yourself. Second, it is in your best interest to stay calm and in control, as well as manage the moods of others around you to help them remain calm and in control.

What You Find Rewarding is not Universal

Many parents offer their partners or children the rewards that they, themselves, would value. More often than not, these rewards are materialistic in nature—a new toy, piece of clothing, or jewelry. These may work in the short term, but parents would do well to determine what their partner or child naturally values. Temperament theory enables the identification of meaningful rewards that family members will truly treasure.

For instance, bear individuals value responsibility, acceptance, and achievement. Tangible rewards that represent hierarchical status, compliance, fulfillment of duty, and responsibility are likely to be prized.

Bears also celebrate history and tradition. Large social gatherings such weddings, reunions, graduations, and—yes—even funerals are important markers of time and achievement.

Ape individuals are looking for recognition for their skills and prowess, so physical items such trophies and certificates related to winning or achieving a physical milestone will mean more. Also, simple validation of their skills will likely be meaningful and motivational for them. The best rewards for apes center around new challenges and experiences.

Dolphins are consumed by relationships and human potential. The best ways to reward them are by arranging for experiences that promote relationships, or thanking them for helping you to achieve your potential. Spending time with dolphins and sharing about yourself are rewards in themselves.

Most owls will have a natural thirst for knowledge and competency. The best rewards for them are opportunities to gather more knowledge, such as visiting places that are repositories (museums with various themes are at the top of the list).

Owls also enjoy opportunities to travel, learning about history and culture.

Many years ago, a course was offered to some of us college students leading up to a youth orchestra tour to the country of Israel. The course explored the history of Masada, the famous stronghold near the Dead Sea, that was built by Herod as one of his cities of escape.

The site became famous when a group of Jewish insurrectionists captured the stronghold from a Roman garrison and nearly withstood a lengthy siege by the Roman Army to recapture it, led by Lucius Silva. When we visited the landmark, I enjoyed knowing details about this ancient historical site (I'm an owl).

Many adults also value collections of various kinds. The type of collection says a great deal about the temperament of the collector. Collections provide wonderful conversation starters, as well other forms of validation and common ground. An added bonus is the need to travel somewhere in an effort to grow the collection.

So Who Are You?

At this point, you should be fairly certain to which temperament family you belong and, hopefully, with which of the 16 temperaments you most identify.

You can also recognize temperament characteristics in those around you, giving you a major advantage in managing your environment and predicting behavior.

Keep in mind that your temperament characteristics are positioned on a continuum: if you are not situated at a pole, your tendencies may not be as obvious.

Also remember that temperament only makes up half of one's personality. Our experiences interact—and collide in some instances—with our temperaments to help create who we are *at this moment in time.*

The Greatest Enemy of Relationships

Family relationships often come with expectations. Unfortunately, expectations often lead to disappointment. The more our experiences differ from our expectations, the more we will struggle with accepting others.

Expectations provide a major impediment to successful and long-lasting relationships. While our basic human instinct is to defensively prejudge a new person or situation, our assumptions are typically crude, hasty, and rarely accurate or predictive *(even though they could be lifesaving).* The simple act of considering everyone you meet as a clean slate will help to curb the natural tendency to prejudice.

Concrete – 74% *(tangible)*
All Bear and Apes

Extrovert – 66% *(outgoing)*
Supervisor + Provider Bears
Promoter + Performer Apes
Teacher + Champion Dolphins
Fieldmarshal + Inventor Owls

Sensing – 74% *(practical)*
All Bears and Apes

Thinking – 52% *(the head)*
Supervisor + Inspector Bears
Promoter + Crafter-Warrior Apes | All Owls

Judging – 53% *(close-ended, resolved)*
All Bears and Owls

What Are the Odds?

Abstract – 26% *(unseen World)*
All Dolphins and Owls

Introvert – 34% *(reserved)*
Inspector + Protector Bears
Crafter-Warrior + Composer Apes
Counselor + Healer Dolphins
Mastermind + Architect Owls

Intuition – 26% *(creative)*
All Dolphins and Owls

Feeling – 48% *(the heart)*
Provider + Protector Bears
Performer + Composer Apes | All Dolphins

Perceiving – 47% *(open-ended, pending)*
All Apes and Dolphins

The Limbic System

People everywhere are increasingly near the boiling point at any given moment. The slightest provocation may send them into a state of emotional hyper-reactivity.

Take road rage for instance. A driver makes an aggressive move—or one that is *perceived* by another driver as aggressive. The second driver is faced with a decision: become irritated and react, or just move on.

In far too many cases, the second driver chooses to retaliate. Perhaps the workday was stressful or sitting in traffic has taken its toll.

Whatever the reason, driver two responds. They go back and forth for a while, with each escalation more radical and dangerous.

The same emotions that flow in the boxing ring or brutal cage-fight are likely boiling over. Two drivers become locked in a fight to the death. *Kill or be killed.*

This same scenario plays out anywhere—in the stands of an arena or stadium, in line at the supermar-

Limbic	Cerebral
Reactive	**Intelligent**

ket, or especially watching one's child play competitive sports. As emotion grows, intelligence diminishes. It is an inverse ratio.

Poor decisions are made. Actions are taken. Regrets ensue once emotions subside. Damages—emotional and even physical—have likely taken place and will need to be repaired.

What is happening? How can intelligent people who are loving and kind around their family members, generous at church, or volunteering to serve the homeless turn into human weapons?

The answers lie in understanding the Limbic System, an area of the human brain that has much to do with subconscious emotions, traumatic memories, and instinctual behaviors.

Most emotions can be categorized within five areas: joy, sadness, fear, anger, and disgust. These emotions are essential to being human. But problems ensue when our emotions sabotage our decisions and actions.

By understanding temperament theory, you take the first step toward learning to deescalate emotional hyper-reactivity—what I call "limbic storms."

Our limbic system is the origin of our primitive, instinctual emotions and behaviors.

Like a newly hatched sea turtle, who makes a desperate dash across the sand in order to evade the sea gulls and other predators, we are programmed with instincts in order to survive as a species. Hunger is another example of a limbic response. Other not-so-frequent examples include the fight-flight-hide instinct, rage, and sensuality.

All of these are legitimate responses, designed to help our species survive and thrive.

While there are a number of opinions among scientists regarding exactly which brain structures should be included as part of the Limbic System, the majority agree on the five structures illustrated on the left.

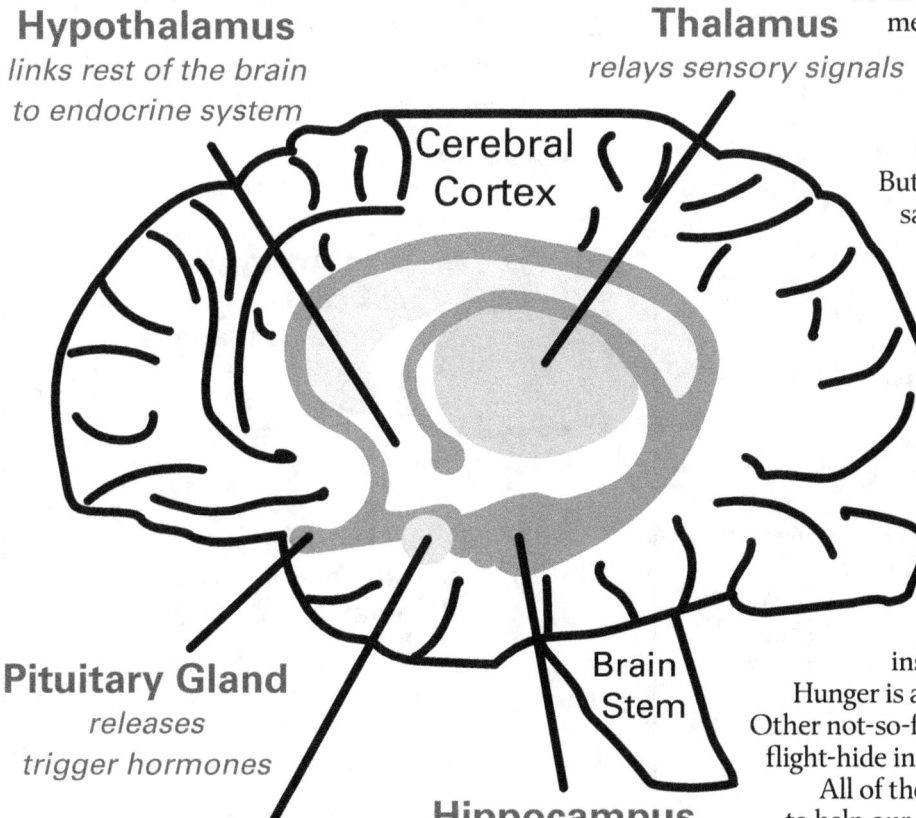

Hypothalamus
links rest of the brain to endocrine system

Thalamus
relays sensory signals

Cerebral Cortex

Pituitary Gland
releases trigger hormones

Brain Stem

Hippocampus
converts short-term memory into long-term

Amygdala
stores memories and connects them to senses, emotions

The **hypothalamus** links the rest of the brain to the endocrine system.

The **pituitary gland** releases hormones that trigger various bodily functions. For instance, adrenocortico-tropic hormone stimulates the adrenal glands to secrete steroidal hormones—principally cortisol—preparing you to fight, flee, or hide in the face of imminent danger.

Two **amygdalae**—one on each side—are responsible for emotions, moods, survival instincts, and memory.

The **hippocampus** transfers short-term memories into long-term and helps us navigate. It also ties our senses and emotions to memories—including traumas.

The **thalamus** relays sensory and motor signals to the cerebral cortex, as well as regulates sleep, consciousness, and alertness.

Limbic Responses

Think for a moment about the primary instincts that motivate animal behavior: self-preservation, food, and reproduction. Most animals spend virtually every waking moment searching for food or water for themselves or their young; fleeing, hiding from, or fighting predators or rivals; courting potential mates or being courted; and protecting their young.

At our core, we human beings must satisfy these same basic needs before we can address the more human needs (see "Hierarchy of Needs" on page 46).

When our emotions boil within us—either positively or negatively—we are likely experiencing our limbic system.

For example, the search for pure bliss is to blame for many addictions. People literally give up food and deny other human needs in order to experience the high of an illicit drug and momentary escape from reality.

When we are face to face with imminent danger, our flee-hide-fight instincts kick in. We quickly choose to make our stand, run, or hide from danger.

Ironically, long-term stress and anxiety release many of the same hormones as flee-hide-fight. Our bodies stand at the ready for imminent danger, even though we are merely experiencing chronic stress.

Remaining indefinitely at high alert wears down our minds and bodies until they ultimately collapse and fail. *For that reason alone*, it is worthwhile to learn how to control our limbic responses, as well as manage those around us.

The Limbic Storm

Like clouds that build during the heat of a summer day, reaching high and turning into monstrous sources of energy, *limbic storms* are the result of a cascade of events. At any point in the process, the storm could dissipate for any number of reasons.

For human beings, the power of choice is a critical

The Limbic Cascade

1. Feelings, twinges
(realistic or distorted perceptions)
Walk away   Engage
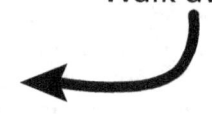

2. Supporting thoughts/images
(perceptions are mentally amplified)
Walk away   Engage
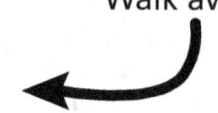

3. Feelings/Emotions intensify
(hormones like adrenaline flood the body)
Walk away   Engage
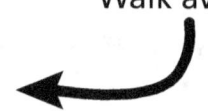

4. Take Action
(fight, flight, or flee takes over)
Walk away   Engage

5. ... Retaliation
(fully limbic, reactive, non-cerebral)
Walk away   Engage
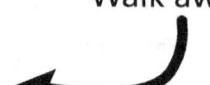

repeat last step
until somebody "dies"
or a participant returns
to cerebral mode

factor. They may choose to take the next step, allowing their emotions to escalate. As their state of reactivity intensifies, it becomes harder to back down and exit.

A limbic response requires a trigger. Knowing the various temperament families and what they value—or despise—provides important clues about what triggers their limbic responses. Along the same lines, you now have insight into how to deescalate limbic behavior.

Here are examples of potential limbic triggers:

- **Fear, intimidation.** Someone threatens you with physical, verbal, and/or emotional posturing.
- **Disrespect.** Someone suggests, through words or actions, that he or she feels superior and does not consider your feelings to be important, or perhaps loses or misuses something that belongs to you.
- **Jealousy, betrayal.** Someone discards a relationship with you, showing preference for another, or shares confidential facts with a third party.
- **Lack of appreciation.** Someone fails to notice an action or effort done out of love or as a favor, or value you as a person.
- **Desire, lust.** You have intense feelings or infatuation for someone or something, leading you toward irresponsible and regrettable actions.

Whatever the motivation, limbic triggers can lead us down treacherous paths where we can inflict major—often irreversible—damage to ourselves and others.

Limbic Storms Are Legitimate Responses

Children often react to their world in limbic fashion. *No wonder!* Their worlds are populated by those who are taller, stronger, and more intimidating.

Their limbic systems are *vital* to their survival. However, it is hoped that mentors will emulate healthy adult behavior, teaching them reason over reaction.

A wide spectrum of adults emerge from childhood with a vastly varying range of skills that guide their behaviors. Some routinely dip into limbic behavior, exhibiting short-fused, moody, or unstable reactions. Others discover ways to remain unrattled, stay cerebral, and maintain their IQ and reason.

For example, at a kids' baseball game, parents are seated around the edge of the field (in lawn chairs or stands), cheering on their 9-year-olds. Some parents remind themselves that this is only a game, that their children are observing their adult behaviors, and that young people need to see examples of the spirit of sportsmanship (cerebral). While they encourage their children to give maximum effort, they also provide emotional support when mistakes are made and the team falls short.

Other parents push their children to win at any cost, yelling at and traumatizing them, questioning and taunting officials, criticizing coaches if the team fails, or accusing the other team of cheating (limbic).

In far too many cases, parents have actually come to blows at their children's ballgames.

Extreme behaviors of any type are harmful to healthy human relationships. Ironically, the ability to control emotion is a powerful predictor of IQ and wealth in populations around the world. More volatile societies tend to display lower IQs and less wealth.

It is possible to learn ways to both self-soothe and deescalate volatile emotions in others.

In the limbic cascade example on the opposite

Behaviors in Others That May Trigger Limbic Responses

Disloyalty, rule-breaking
Disrespect for authority
Ignoring the tried and true
Disrespecting tradition
Belittling rank and status
Laziness, shirking duty

Inaction, obstruction
Drawn out and boring
Too old-fashioned
Too many rules
Inflexibility, inertia
Fear, timidity, clumsiness

Unkind, unsympathetic
Insincere, thoughtless
Bullying, impulsive
Lacking team spirit
Impatient, rude
Lack of planning
Selfish

Incompetence, unskilled
Brash, lacking insight
Conceited, non-strategic
Ignoring consequences
Unintelligent, impulsive
Belittling, embarrassing
Unfair, unjust

page, either participant could choose to exit the cascade at any point.

However, as emotional temperatures rise, it becomes increasingly unlikely that either will exit—even though injury and destruction are inevitable.

Staying Cerebral in the Heat of Conflict

A number of techniques may be employed to deescalate a limbic storm. The simplest is to not participate—*to not engage.*

When a child becomes heated and reactive, a parent will often take him or her to a quiet, secluded area to cool off. The child is in "time-out." Adults are able to decide the same—to remove themselves from a situation in order to cool down. This move actually takes more willpower and self-control than staying in the fray—though some mistakenly view it as cowardice.

Following are some strategies for deescalating a limbically charged situation.

- **Stay calm and cerebral.** When people lash out, *it is rarely about you.* Knowing this helps you remain calm and not take it personally.
- **Draw fire.** Ask limbic individuals to explain the situation as well as if you have done something to offend them. Disarm them with humility.
- **Rephrase.** Have them explain the situation, then summarize what you're hearing. Remain calm and positive in your conversation—as if the problem is entirely solvable. Be good-natured and affirming.
- **Validate feelings.** Sympathize with phrases such as "I see what you mean;" empathize with phrases such as "That must be really upsetting;" and normalize with phrases such as "I'm sure you have a reason to be upset." But be careful not to validate limbic speech or behaviors. *They're not okay.*
- **Ask a limbic individual for help.** If you ask for suggestions to solve the perceived problem, you may actually receive some useful advice. What would they suggest? Engage agitants in solving the problem, inviting them to join *Team Solution* rather than *Team Complaint.*

Managing Your Environment

Most people around you have no concept of temperament theory or why they are limbically triggered to become emotionally reactive and uncontrolled.

You do—and now that you have the tools to manage the situation, you can help recenter limbic individuals around you. It is in everyone's best interest for all to remain cerebral and rational.

Out-of-control reactions and behaviors often leave a trail of destruction and require significant repair of relationships and reputations.

Don't let your limbic system run your life. Practice

Soothing and Disarming Phrases to Calm Limbic Storms

"You did a really good job."
"You deserve a rest."
"What can I do to help?"
"You deserve my respect."
"You really have everything
running so smoothly."

"You are so talented."
"How did you do that?"
"You really made a difference."
"Your actions saved the day."
"I love it when you perform."
"You are a mechanical genius."

"You really understand me."
"Thank you for believing in me."
"You're the best friend I could
ever ask for."
"You are so kind and thoughtful."
"You are so unselfish."

"Wow! You're a genius."
"How do you know so much
about everything?"
"That is an amazing idea."
"What could I do differently?"
"You're so good at what you do."

remaining thoughtful, logical, and in control.

In the final chapter, the concept of the Vital Self is introduced, sharing additional ways to maintain control. Internal limbic feelings provide useful clues for identifying personal triggers.

Recognizing and avoiding triggers is an important step toward soothing yourself and others.

Relational Systems

Wherever there are two or more people gathered, a mappable system of interactions is taking place. Family systems theory, first hypothesized in 1988, suggests that the family is a complex collection of components interacting and impacting each other.

Each member of the family system has distinct behavioral patterns in relation to other family members. These patterns can be defined and reshaped by trained family therapists, resulting in system-wide change.

A major theme of this book has made the point that we are all born with certain temperaments which, when combined with human experience, result in our personalities. As a result, it is pointless—and harmful—to try and coerce change in another individual's basic temperament characteristics.

In order to bring about change in others, the best method is to improve oneself. Others will naturally change in how they relate to you—*effectively changing them.* This idea is based upon family systems theory.

Family systems theory has broadened to become systems theory, recognizing that systems of human interaction develop in any setting where two or more people regularly interact. The workplace is one such setting, but the concepts can be applied to any group of humans—since groups take on unique characteristics when they are together.

People can be grouped in many ways: families, societies, races, cultures, genders, organizations, regions, and even countries.

Family Systems

Since the topic of this book is parenting, we will concentrate on family systems. Many suggestions have already been made throughout these pages, and family systems will overlap some of them—but from a systems perspective. Temperament theory works well with systems theory because groups—like individuals—take on certain temperament-style characteristics.

The traditional family system includes a father, mother, and at least one child. A healthy family has a strong parental team that deals kindly but firmly with the children, setting boundaries and communicating roles and expectations.

Alliances. When three or more human beings interact, *they will align with each other* in various ways, depending on the setting and expectations.

Healthy alliances are beneficial to both parties, creating warmth, trust, and understanding. They observe the boundaries of social interaction and intimacy, set by the society or culture in which the participants reside.

Unhealthy alliances become problematic because boundaries are crossed and inappropriate behavior ensues. They typically lead to unfair treatment of a third party.

Triangling. The most basic problematic alliance is triangling—two against one. This is one of the most basic tendencies of human behavior, summed up in the well-known phrase, "two's company, three's a crowd."

If you have any doubts regarding this human tendency, observe three children playing. Invariably, one member of the threesome will be left out with some activity as the other two align.

Behavioral patterns and roles. Particularly in families, patterns of behavior develop over time. These patterns—or roles—are so powerful that many adults find themselves falling back into old patterns when they return to family gatherings, no matter how hard they try to avoid doing so. The family system seems to force them back into immature behaviors reminiscent of their childhood, adolescence, or early adulthood.

Crossing boundaries. There are accepted family boundaries established by various cultures and traditions. In the United States, Judeo-Christian values are still quite prevalent, though there are forces trying to disrupt and destroy them, dissolving the core family, rejecting law and order, accepting the thoughtless and selfish murder of the unborn, encouraging sexual promiscuity, and a host of other threats.

Within the nuclear family, a parental team should never breach the boundaries of involving children in parental disputes and adult issues, nor take part in incestuous relationships with their children. These boundaries, once crossed, cause irreparable harm.

Creating Family Patterns

Parents have the awe-inspiring task of creating the family patterns that will endure for their lives and will impact their descendants indefinitely. Before children are even considered, the parental team needs to reach consensus on everything from finances to raising a family, establishing the basic guidelines and protocols, and committing to following them or privately making adjustments as a parental team.

Failure to do so will result in a weak parental team, easily breached, manipulated, and divided even by a child with average intelligence.

While children may seem to delight in dividing and conquering their parents, their success is deeply disquieting and alarming to them, bringing into question their own security. In other words, children need boundaries, and many will push until they find them.

Relational Continuum

Like the four continua suggested by Myers and Briggs, relationships fall on a continuum of sorts. For this setting, we'll use a temperature-based scale.

Warmest. This relationship is characterized by unconditional love and support. Absolute trust allows for discussion of even the most painful topics with no worries of betrayal or reprisal. However, in the case of a parent and child, consequences may be required but should be meted out in the most loving and forgiving manner. When children are aware of—or even part of deciding—the consequences for various indiscretions, they are more likely to willingly accept them.

Warmer. This relationship is based upon mutual respect, acceptance, and appreciation. While conversations may delve deeply into painful or embarrassing topics, there is clear friendship and support for each other, but a hesitancy to become too intimate.

Warm. This relationship has the aspects of respect and acceptance. However, no efforts are made to spend additional time together than happens naturally during life. Conversations are pleasant, but neither individual really wants to know too much.

Cool. This relationship may show tolerance on the surface but is characterized by a negative undercurrent. These individuals will not make any extra effort to interact and may actually avoid each other when possible. However, they are likely interested enough to hear the latest gossip about the other person.

Cooler. This relationship has some underlying hostility leading participants to avoid contact. Conversations will be few and generally unfriendly. There is likely an incident or two where hostile words were exchanged or unfriendly actions taken.

Cold. This relationship is full of mutual hostility. These individuals should not be in the same room together or an altercation—verbal and/or physical—will almost certainly ensue.

The Value of Models

Models of family systems can be especially useful for family therapists. However, parents may also benefit in addressing relational issues and interactions.

In the family system model below, here are facts we can draw from the illustration:

• Mom and Dad have a strong relationship.

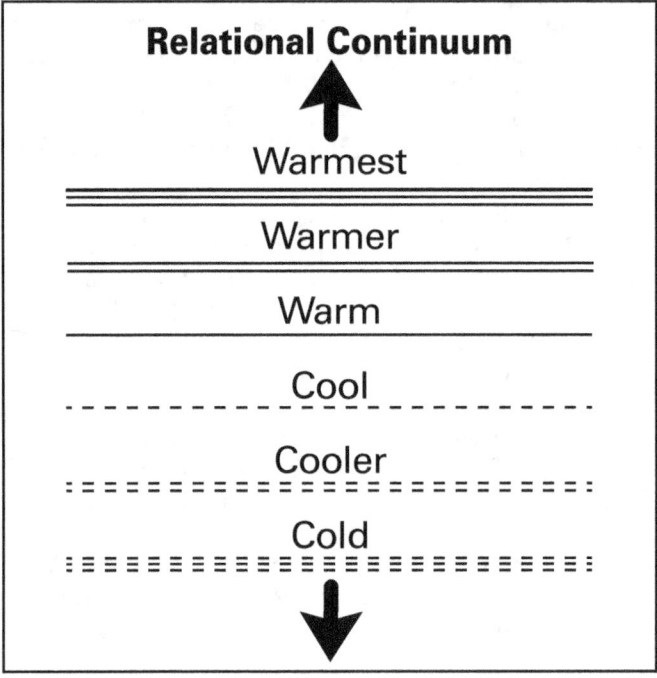

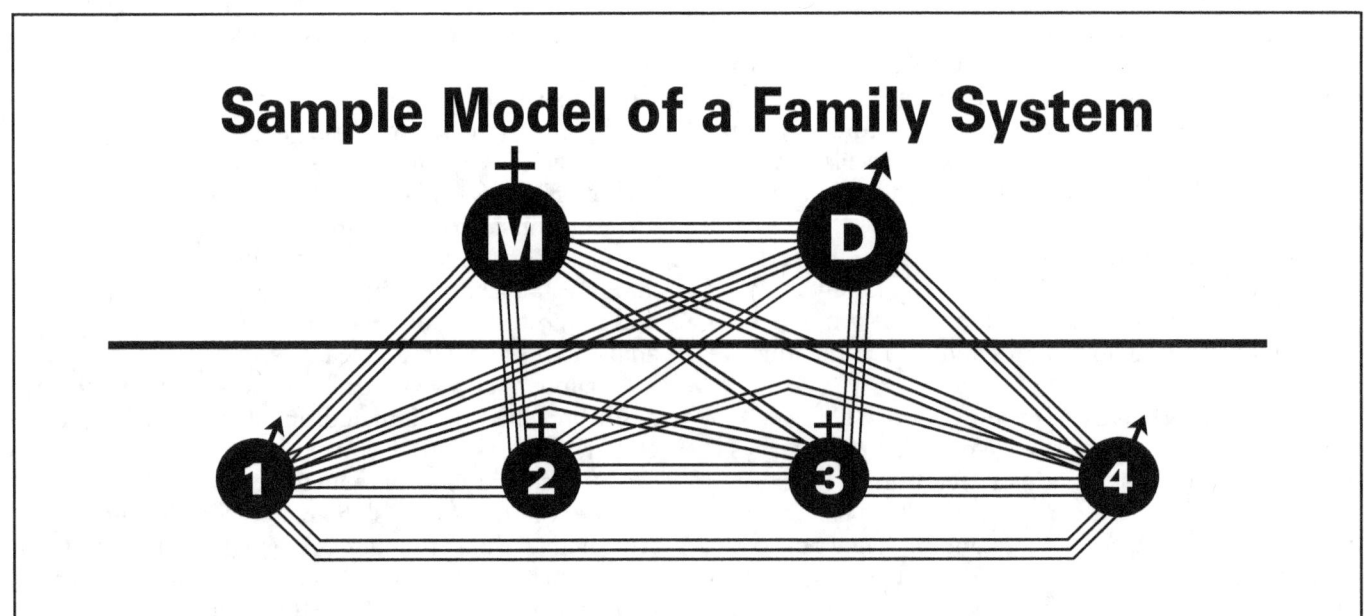

- Mom is the closest to the oldest son and daughter, as well as the youngest son. She is not quite as close to the youngest daughter.
- Dad is closest to the oldest son as well as the youngest daughter and son. He is a not as close to the oldest daughter.
- The oldest son is not quite as close to the oldest daughter, but is closer to his other siblings.
- The oldest daughter is not as close to either of her brothers but is closer to her other sister.
- The youngest daughter is close to all three of her siblings, suggesting she is the warmer of the two daughters.
- The youngest son is closer to his older brother and sister nearest in age to him, while not so close to his older sister.

The next step in the process is to account for the variations in warmth among the siblings. A typical reason for less closeness is competition—for achievement or for the attention of one or more of the parents.

The simple process of looking at the model is therapeutic by itself, since the parents are able to address deficits and create opportunities to remedy them—utilizing one-to-one discussions, shared activities, and a host of other strategies.

Problematic Family Relationships

The remainder of this chapter will discuss family systems where problematic relationships occur—either too close and inappropriate or negatively explosive.

Family systems become particularly unbalanced when the following situations occur:

- **Unbalanced parental team.** One partner dominates the family, making all of the decisions and cutting the other one off completely. In many cases, the dominated parent is treated as one of the children through behaviors and comments.
- **Parent/child alliances.** When parents are different temperaments, and they have children who each match one parent more than the other, alliances naturally occur. Most children will admit they are closer to one parent than the other. Parents, on the other hand, are supposed to be impartial, according to accepted family norms. Alliances become unhealthy when they weaken other relationships in the family. For instance, a child may become an emotional substitute for the spouse and—in cases of incest—sexually involved.
- **Devouring mother and raging father.** The devouring mother will consciously or unconsciously create a barrier around her children to protect them the world—keeping them in an infantile state. This is increasingly common in today's world. The resulting adult infants are

prevalent in many of the younger generations today. The raging father, a traditional archetype, dominates the family through angry intimidation and shaming, thwarting the emotional health and development of both wife and children.

- **White sheep, black sheep.** In some cases, parents of similar temperaments will revere a child that is similar to them in temperament, while rejecting a child who is a different temperament. Often, the rejected child will exercise the defenses of victimhood or opposition. This creates the black sheep scenario, and many of the family's problems are attributed to this child.
- **Middle-child syndrome.** In families with more than two children, there is always a middle child. For most families, their hopes and dreams are pinned upon the oldest child, and their youngest remains the "baby"—coddled emotionally and physically into adulthood. Middle children miss out on these natural roles. Many attempt to overachieve to be noticed, or simply fade into the background of the family system.
- **Spoiled child.** As a rule, the most spoiled children are either an only child or the baby of the family. Instead of the devouring mother keeping them in permanent infancy, both parents participate in this major disservice. Spoiled children typically lack resiliency because their parents have always stepped in to save them.
- **Helicopter parents.** In recent years, the term "helicopter parent" has been coined to describe parents who literally hover over their children, interceding to save them from any of life's consequences. The resulting adult infants who wilt under any pressure—also know as "snowflakes"—are typical of many young people today who are victims of the "woke" culture.
- **Lawnmower parents.** Rather than being reactive like helicopter parents, lawnmower parents take initiative and prepare the way for their children so that their lives are smooth and worry-free. Again, the result is an infant adult.

Avoiding Problematic Relationships

Parents have the awesome task of guiding and shaping their children in ways that will sustain them into adulthood, parenthood, and beyond. Seemingly unimportant decisions they make today in raising their children will have repercussions that could last for multiple generations.

As a parent, *you will make mistakes,* and some will be harmful and lasting. The first step is arm yourself with knowledge and wisdom—which you are doing at this very moment as you read this book.

The second is to admit your mistakes and discuss them with your parental partner, developing strategies to counter them. Admitting your mistakes to your children must be carefully done, since you do not want to weaken the parental team. However, an apologetic parent is a powerful example to provide for your children.

In the next chapter, the importance of honestly admitting your mistakes, shortcomings, and weaknesses are a critical part of being honest with yourself and others. Admission and acceptance of responsibility should now lead to cleaning up the messes you make.

The third is to stick with your strategies to not only counter mistakes but set new directions for your family system of relationships.

Part of resiliency is not being devastated when you make a mistake. You can reframe your mistakes in the following ways:

• You tested and ruled out one approach.
• Your mistakes remind you that you are a human being prone to mistake-making. However, you clean up your mistakes and create strategies and protocols to avoid the same mistakes later.
• Mistakes provide you the opportunity to model humility, honesty, and resiliency to your children, showing them how to pick up the pieces and continue on.

Most children innately trust behaviors and actions far more than words. Congruence between words and actions is one of the best ways to model honesty and integrity. The phrase, "actions speak louder than words," perfectly sums up this life fact.

Examining the Devouring Mother Family System

In contrast to the fairly healthy family system mod-eled on page 40, the system below is highly disturbing and will almost certain result in children who remain infants well into their adulthood.

Keep in mind that adult children who remain in the parental home well into their mid-20s and beyond typically lack the confidence to face the world on their own. They intrinsically know when their life skills are underdeveloped and untried. That makes the future daunting and terrifying.

Parents should provide decision-making opportunities for their children and allow them to suffer consequences. While children are not innately prepared to make wise choices on their own, parents can still present safe options and allow the child to choose.

In the family system below, note that the "parental" boundary only exists between the mother and father, and that the father is at a reduced level of influence and importance within the family system.

In addition, the mother has unhealthy relationships with her children—entangled ones where the children are not allowed to develop their own identity. Also note that one child has defied the mother's hatred toward Dad. Few children are able and willing to stand up to a devouring mother.

A wise therapist would also suspect unhealthy physical relations and even sexual abuse—most likely between the mother and oldest son who has become an emotional substitute for the emasculated father.

Much like a white board used by a football or basketball coach during a game, the family system model can be used to not only discover and point out problem relationships, but also help restore the family system to higher levels of function. After all, family patterns lay the groundwork for the rest of the children's lives.

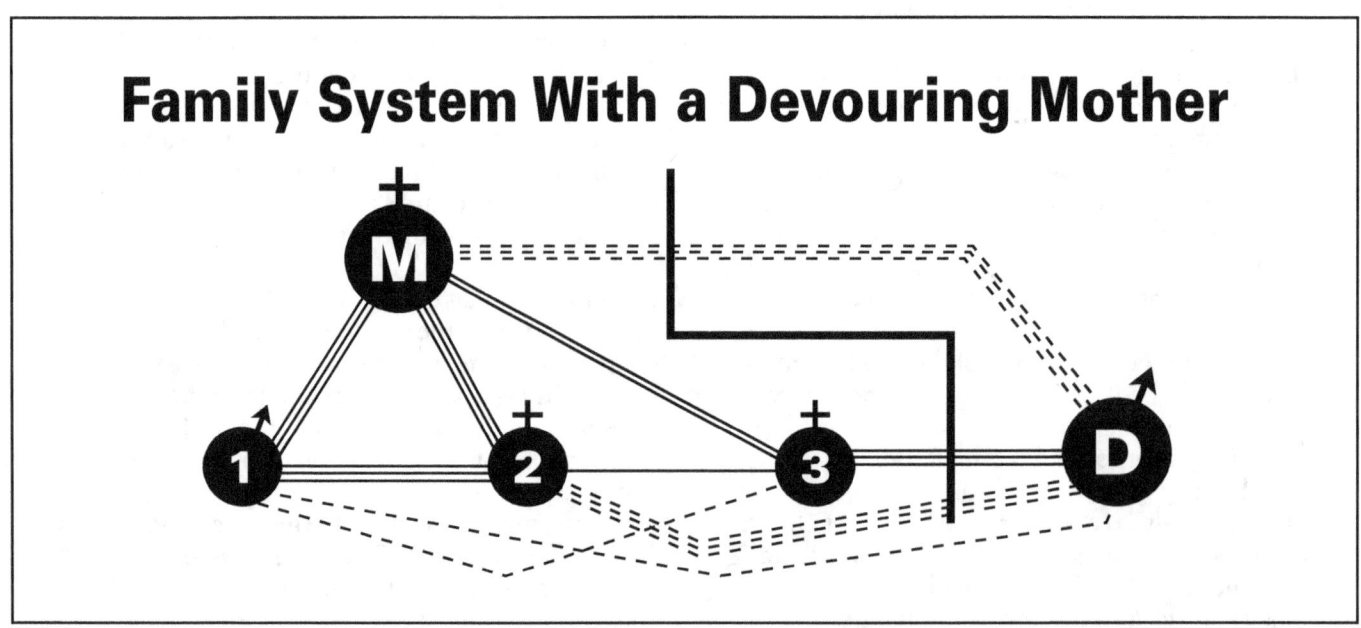

Family System With a Devouring Mother

The Vital Self

There are certain "tells" that give it away when someone is experiencing a limbic storm. From giddy to raging, limbic behavior covers a full spectrum of emotions.

The IQ disappears. There is no chance of being thoughtful or reasonable. The only option—aside from reacting with limbic abandon and destroying your reputation—is to soothe yourself or someone around you. Once calm is restored, the IQ will reappear.

However, be warned: never tell a person who is in the midst of a limbic storm to "calm down." Limbic individuals are typically *incapable* of calming themselves. Such words only fuel their emotional meltdowns.

Many limbic outbursts are examples of defensive behavior. When an individual feels emotionally threatened, he or she will often resort to defensive behaviors that are typical of children and instinctive by nature.

Along similar lines, when an individual is trying change, coerce, or manipulate others, he or she will often turn to familiar and harmful relational tools that have been employed over millennia.

In the following paragraphs, I refer to these two groups of behaviors as "Critical Parenting" and "Childhood Defenses."

Critical parenting can be summarized under three categories: intimidation, guilting, and shaming. Likewise, childhood defenses include compliance, victimhood, and opposition.

Critical Parenting

The term "parenting" can be misleading because parents aren't the only ones to use intimidation, guilt, or shaming to manipulate and coerce. And not all parents resort to these relational techniques.

There is a clear difference between this first technique of critical parenting, **intimidation,** and simply establishing a system of consequences for unacceptable behaviors, then following through.

The primary difference lies in the consistency of the consequences, as well as the spirit in which they are meted out.

Punishment dispatched in anger is never appropriate. In fact, replacing the term "punishment" with "consequences" goes a long way in describing the major contrasts between critical and healthy parenting.

Intimidation often occurs for selfish reasons. A child misbehaving in public can be a major source of embarrassment for a parent. In fact, the child is likely aiming for that very result, trying to manipulate the parent into meeting a demand.

Success for the child is achieved when the parent either gives in to the demands or reacts negatively. There are no winners if a parent loses control and becomes physically or verbally abusive.

Guilting is a second critical parenting technique. The phrase, "I'm so disappointed in you," is a good example. Shame on the child, colleague, friend, or acquaintance who fails to do what is demanded. Spouses may say, "If you really loved me, you would … ." In some cultures, embarrassment of an entire family is used to coerce a family member into a prescribed behavior—*guilting him or her into compliance.*

A third technique of manipulation is **shaming.** Essentially, this is name-calling. Labeling a family member, colleague, or friend as lazy or stupid falls within this category. Such labels are attempts to humiliate or intimidate others into submission.

Children have been told that they are good for nothing, stupid, imbeciles, retarded, and far worse. Damage caused by such labeling is long-lasting.

Techniques that rely on manipulation or coercion are fundamentally faulty, eroding the God-given power of choice for others.

Shaming, intimidation, and guilting have no valid place in adult interactions—toward children or other adults. They are based on the premise that one human being can force change upon another.

Childhood Defenses

The vulnerability of children causes them to be especially reliant upon their defenses. They have legitimate reasons to be concerned! They can be overpowered by most adults around them. Their personal safety is *literally at risk.*

Children employ three primary defenses: compliance, victimhood, and opposition. Along with critical parenting techniques, many adults take childhood defenses with them into adulthood.

These behaviors are most often encountered when an individual escalates into a limbic state, relying on primitive human instincts.

Compliance is the most common. When children are forced to comply through intimidation, guilting, or shaming, they are damaged as human beings. Unhealthy reasons for compliance include fear, seeking to please, and self-loathing. Compliant children easily give up their personal freedom.

Some overly compliant adults are labeled as co-dependent, with every aspect of their identity and existence wrapped up in the will, behavior, and identity of another. Family members of addicts facilitate an addiction by covering it up and pretending everything is perfectly normal. "Nothing to see here."

Victimhood is a second common defense, allowing people to wait for others to act, rather than taking responsibility for their own actions. They may not realize that playing victim simply means giving away their power *by expecting and waiting for others to change.*

Our society is replete with victims, sitting idly by and waiting for others to improve their situations, taking no responsibility whatsoever for themselves.

There are legitimate victims. However, most victims are fully capable of rising above their situations and removing themselves from harm's way.

But it takes effort. People find it far easier to complain and wallow in their victimhood.

Opposition is a third defense. Pushed to their limits, some children become defiant and lash out at their perceived oppressors. Driven by rage, they are labeled by others as hot-tempered, unstable, and short-fused.

Their opposition may take the form of verbal or physical warfare. Or they may choose to self-mutilate —rings or studs in various body parts, tattoos, or even self-harm such as cutting themselves.

Children grow into adults. Rage and defiance remain near the surface, ready to explode at the slightest trigger or provocation.

Interplay of Defenses

On the facing page is an illustration of a healthy Vital Self. Notice that the three critical parents and three defensive children are all shown as satellites orbiting and speaking to the Vital Self—the inner adult voice that is supported by the inner council.

This model explains the components of the Vital Self, working together to enable an individual to remain the calmest, smartest person in the room.

The illustration on page 47 exemplifies a limbic response where traumatic memories trigger the limbic system and activate the Intimidating Critical Parent— now speaking on behalf of the sleeping Vital Self. These types of internal scenarios result in limbic outbursts.

In this example, a critical parent is threatening the recipient with dire consequences, speaking in place of the Vital Self as well as attacking a defensive child.

Relationships between parent and child, or between spouses, other family members, friends, or colleagues are likely to be damaged. Harmful words and actions can never be retrieved.

Creating the Vital Self

Vitality can be defined a number of ways: full of life, healthy, strong, impervious to conflict, feeling valued, and emotionally secure.

Creating a Vital Self will allow you to weather life, remain truthful to yourself and others, and avoid partic-

ipating in pointless and harmful limbic exchanges.

Those who choose to simply withdraw suffer extreme loneliness, and for good reason: others sense when they want to be left alone.

Face-to-face human interaction has been scientifically shown to release positive hormones into the body that not only help an individual feel better, but actually build immunity and resiliency against physical and emotional adversity.

The obvious solution, then, is to continue interacting with other human beings—*but in better ways.* Like a puppeteer, you can manage the mood and outcome of most scenarios by remaining calm and cerebral, operating out of your brain's center of reason, as well as helping others to do the same.

The Center

Your vital self is essentially *you acting as an adult,* fully in charge every waking hour. Everyone you encounter will "talk to the adult," who must remain awake and alert.

Your adult voice is supported by a Council of Advisors that you have chosen. They can be anyone—a superhero or a parental figure. You'll need real or imaginary icons on your council to serve as kind critic, coach, cheerleader, strategist, powerful hero, nurturing parent, and so forth. If you are a Christian, your council could include God the Father, Son, and Holy Spirit.

By literally visualizing your council, you will be better able to hear and follow what they have to say.

It is imperative that your adult self control every external conversation.

The Satellites

Ignoring or burying your limbic feelings can be equally detrimental. Buried feelings and emotions will fester and likely re-emerge at some inopportune time.

When you feel tempted to use critical parenting (i.e., intimidating, guilting, or shaming) or childhood defenses (i.e., complying, playing victim, or rebelling), you are sensing a trigger within your environment. Sensitivity toward limbic feelings serves as an early warning system to avoid being triggered.

Your critical parents and defensive children are not to speak directly to anyone outside your inner thoughts. However, their antennae are valuable tools. The moment you feel limbic emotions welling up inside you or an urge to intimidate, guilt, name-call, rage, play victim, or meekly comply, inform your vital self.

You are then able to identify the source of limbic disturbance (yourself included), choose a course of action—depending on your level of control—and self-soothe or perhaps step in to manage and soothe

Continued on page 46

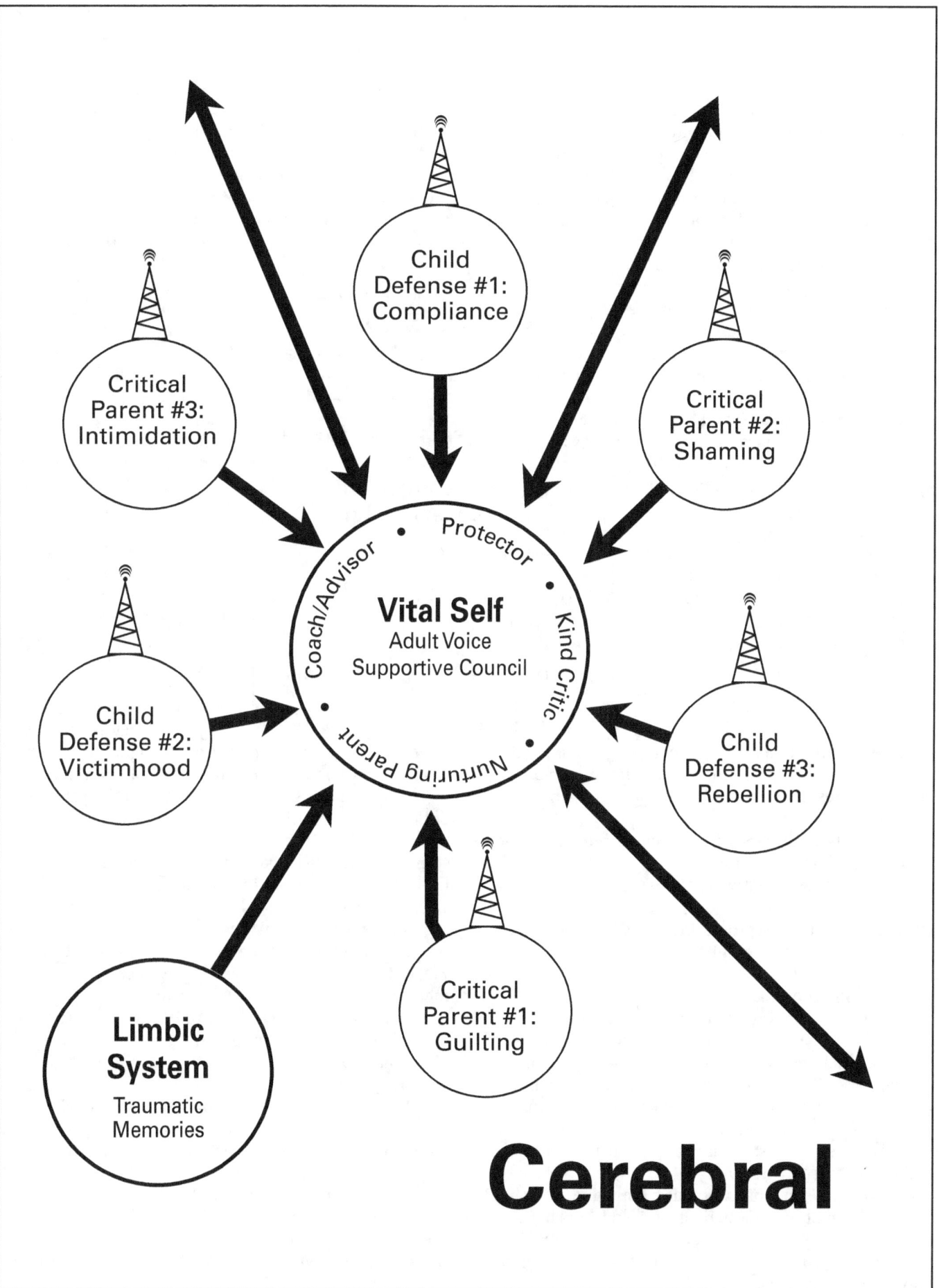

Cerebral

Continued from page 44
another so that his or her IQ may return.

It is always in your best interest to interact with people who are fully cerebral. If you are hoping to have a useful and beneficial conversation, you will want everyone to be calm and in control of their emotions.

PTSD is Far More Common Than You Think

Post-traumatic Stress Disorder, or PTSD, has been used to describe subconscious physical and emotional responses to environmental triggers for soldiers who have experienced wartime horrors.

However, any traumatic experience can result in PTSD for any individual. Whenever a person feels in imminent danger and fears for personal survival and safety, a traumatic memory may be registered by the amygdalae, part of the limbic system, then transferred via the hippocampus into long-term memory.

Since children are by far the most vulnerable members of the human species, they are more likely to acquire traumatic memories due to short- or long-term physical or psychological abuse. A horrifying accident or experience can also sear itself into the memory, causing pure terror, panic, or other strong emotions when triggered.

These memories can be created even before an infant learns to speak, often making it difficult to pinpoint the source. As children grow into adulthood, residual traumatic memories remain and can result in unidentifiable limbic responses.

A variety of therapies have been developed to help process and lessen the emotional impact of past traumas—even those that are pre-verbal.

One such process is known as eye-movement desensitization and reprocessing (EMDR) and is best done with a trained therapist.

The Personal Sanctuary

As a final component of your vital self, you will want to create **your personal sanctuary.** This can be a real or imagined place in your mind that represents peace, tranquility, and safety. It should be somewhere to which you retreat when you feel limbic emotions threatening to overwhelm.

You access your sanctuary and allow your emotional reactivity to melt away.

Here is my personal sanctuary: I imagine a tiny inlet on the North Shore of Kauai, the garden island in the Hawaiian archipelago. A thatched open hut keeps the hot sun at bay, and a cool breeze plays with the emerald waves that crash beyond and lap at the sand.

I sip my favorite beverage, a virgin piña colada, with its sweet pineapple, coconut froth, and crushed ice. My toes dig into the cool, moist sand at the water's edge. This is my escape when intense emotions threaten to pull me into a limbic state of mind.

Create your own slice of paradise, wherever that might be. Go there often.

In this illustration, Abraham Maslow's "Hierarchy of Needs" suggests that human beings cannot begin to address higher needs until the basic ones are met. For instance, an individual who does not feel safe and secure, who is hungry or thirsty, or seriously sleep-deprived will not be concerned with self-esteem, accomplishment, love, or belonging until he or she feels safe and secure, has satiated both hunger and thirst, and is well-rested.

Along the same lines, when you experience traumatic memories, you may become emotionally and developmentally frozen in time, unable to progress to higher levels of self-awareness, self-esteem, and self-enlightenment.

In the previous section, the therapeutic technique of EMDR was mentioned. While it is best to work with a certified clinical therapist in using this technique, some benefit may be gained through self-administered EMDR. To accomplish this, you need to find a YouTube video that has both visual and audio components.

For some unknown reason, following a moving dot on a screen with your eyes, while listening to a tone that moves from ear to ear, may help you access traumatic memories and lessen their limbic impact.

To try self-administered EMDR, you will need a pair of headphones and a computer. A good EMDR YouTube video may be found at: https://www.youtube.com/watch?v=DALbwI7m1vM

As you watch and listen to the video, you will need to do the following: 1) visualize your traumatic memory, situation, or emotions as a floating satellite; 2) picture a rope ladder between the satellite and your personal sanctuary; 3) imagine yourself going down the ladder toward your painful feelings or emotions, then retreating to your sanctuary when the emotions threaten to overwhelm you; and 4) you should be able

Continued on page 48

Self-Fulfillment Needs
- Achievement
- Creativity

Psychological Needs
- Self-esteem
- Accomplishment
- Love, Belonging

Basic Needs
- Safety
- Security
- Food, Water, Warmth, Rest

Abraham Maslow's "Hierarchy of Needs"

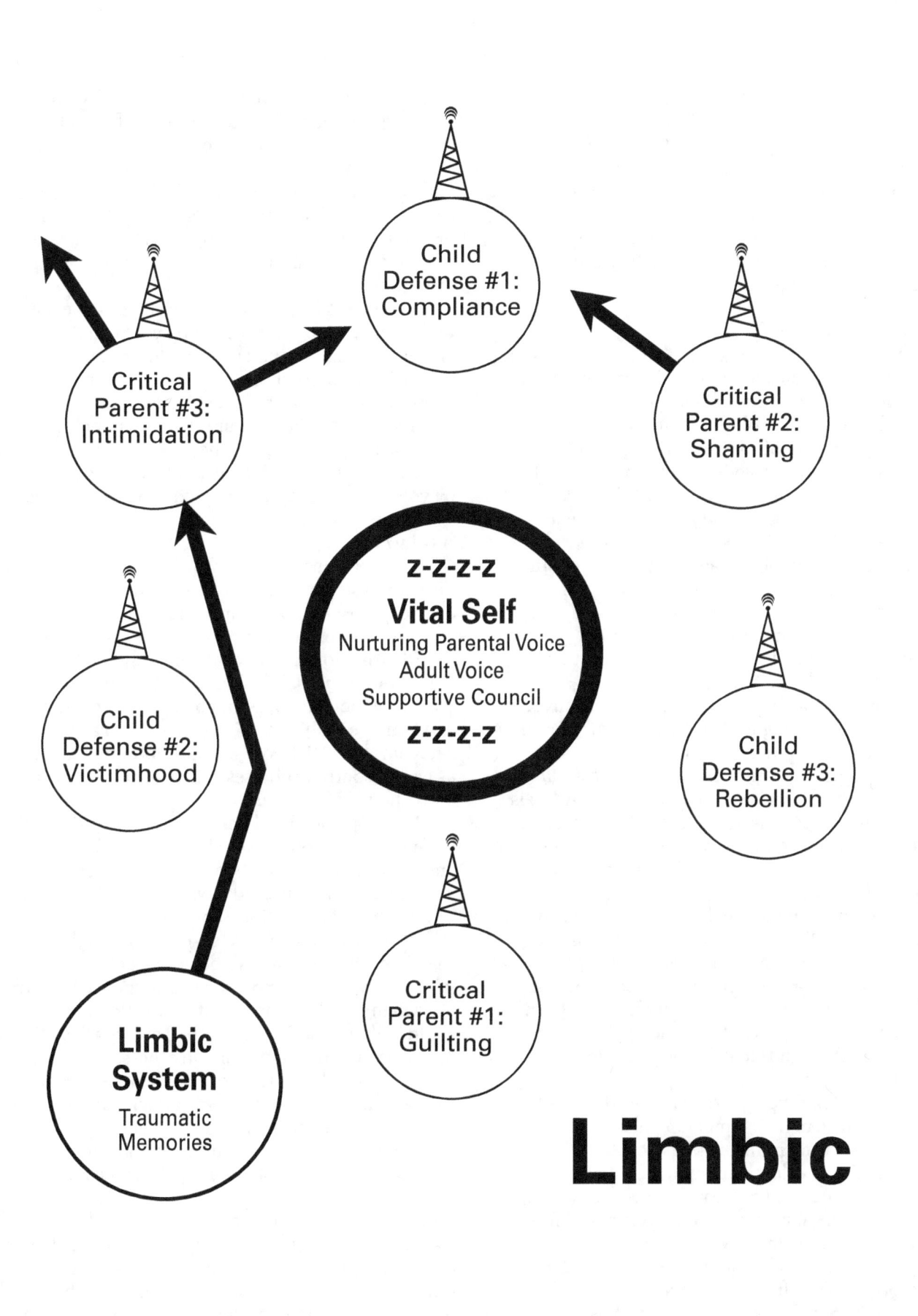

Limbic

Continued from page 46
to spend longer periods of time "in the pain" as you become desensitized to the traumatic memories, emotions, and associated discomfort.

Using EMDR with a trained therapist does not work for everyone; self-administered EMDR will likely be similar. But, it may be worth a try if you have painful memories or feelings that derail you (such as unease, fear, anxiety, or even panic).

Rules for The Vital Self

Remember, growing your vital self requires learning to manage your limbic emotions and reactions in order to become a better person. To build your vital self, you must establish some **absolute ground rules** that you incorporate into your life. For example:

Rule 1: Be **absolutely honest** with yourself and others. When you mess up, own it. *(When you lie to yourself, your world is forever shifting and unstable.)*

Rule 2: You must **always clean up your messes** when you dip into limbic behavior. Apologize profusely to those you have harmed and beg their forgiveness. Humbly tell them that you behaved poorly and are working toward becoming a better person.

If you're anything like me, your discomfort will discourage future limbic outbursts—*all good.*

Rule 3: Your satellites **may never speak** to anyone outside your own thoughts. Let them rage in your mind until they lose their power and momentum.

Rule 4: Your adult self must practice *selfish enlightenment,* always asking about every situation, "**What is in *my* best interest?**" It is *never* in your best interest to lose control and make a mess of your relationships.

Tying It All Together

Temperament theory helps you understand and appreciate yourself and others around you, lessening the tendency to look down on others or berate yourself.

Rather than being self-critical, you seek to understand your natural tendencies. When they lead to challenges such as making friends or holding down a job, you create workarounds to help you thrive in a world dominated by bears.

Second, when others become limbic, the keys to soothing them lie in their temperaments. Each temperament craves certain phrases (see page 42), and when you use them, you calm their limbic outbursts.

Naturally, you need to mean what you say and back your words with supporting actions. *Never* tell limbic individuals to "just calm down."

Third, many are oblivious to the fact they cannot change others. They fruitlessly hope to "improve" a spouse, child, friend, colleague, or even a boss.

The process of trying to change others will require

manipulation and coercion—intimidating, guilting, and shaming—forcing others to comply, defy, or play victim. Results are unpredictable at best.

The ideal way to change other people is to improve yourself. When you change for the better, you create a ripple effect that impacts everyone in your sphere of influence. Others will change in relation to you—whether they realize it or not. In this sense, you *can* change others.

There certainly will be complicated conversations taking place in your head, helping you manage thoughts and emotions that could take you to bad places.

Let your internal conversations happen, but *never* allow others to hear them. The conversations between you and your satellites, your personal council, and your vital self are private. Everyone you encounter and with whom you interact will now *talk to the vital self,* backed by your wise council and warned by your satellites.

A New Process

Relationships, wherever they take place, represent intricate systems of actions and reactions, emotions and counter-emotions, words and responses. To help you navigate relationships, follow this process:

Identify, tolerate, accept, and appreciate temperament differences. The diversity of the people around you make them unique—not bad, wrong, or stupid.

Manage limbic reactivity inside and around you. Knowing what "ticks off" the various temperaments, as well as soothing phrases, will help you calm yourself and others around you.

Develop your Vital Self. By organizing the various components of your vital self—your council, satellites, and personal sanctuary—you create a better way to stay within your cerebral mind as well as avoid limbic-based feelings, emotions, actions, and reactions.

Those within your circle "speak to the adult," rather than your critical parent or defensive child.

Your limbic "feelings" serve as antennae to warn you when people in the vicinity are thinking or behaving in limbic fashion. You are then able to manage reactivity within yourself and in others.

Own your behavior. Be brutally honest with yourself and others regarding your behavior. When you mess up, own it and apologize.

Recognize the feelings and emotions that threaten to boil over. Take time to regroup, letting your adult self reassure and soothe the defensive child or tell the critical parent to "stand down."

Without realizing exactly why, people will feel safer around you because of your situational awareness, inner calm, and positivity. They, in turn, will become more calm, honest, open, and cerebral in your presence, bringing peace to your corner of the world.

A Glossary of Terms

Abstract:	Focused on ideas, concepts, theories, and intuition.
Apes:	Temperament family, shares sensing and perceiving (SP). *Themes: freedom and impact.*
Bears:	Temperament family, shares sensing and judging (SJ). *Themes: responsibility and duty.*
Briggs, Katharine Cook:	Mother of Isabel Briggs Myers. Together, they created the Myers-Briggs system to determine and describe temperaments.
Childhood Defenses:	Reactions to critical parenting. Includes complying, playing victim, and opposing.
Concrete:	Focused on the present, the five senses, and factual details.
Continua:	Ranges between the polar opposites of extroversion vs. introversion, sensing vs. intuition, thinking vs. feeling, and judging vs. perceiving.
Critical Parenting:	The use of intimidation, shaming, and guilting to manipulate others.
Dolphins:	Temperament family, shares intuition and feeling (NF). *Themes: relationships and human potential.*
Extrovert:	Talkative, outgoing, prefers fast-paced environment, thinks out loud, and enjoys attention.
Feeling:	Value-based decisions, enables others, harmony, forgiveness, pleasing, and support.
Guilting:	Linking a requested response to damaging personal or family reputation.
Hippocrates:	Famous philosopher *circa* 450 B.C. who wrote about choleric, phlegmatic, melancholic, and sanguine temperament types.
Introvert:	Reserved, private, prefers slower thoughtful pace, comfortable with self, and observant.
Intuition:	Impressions, big picture, creativity, innovation, interpretation, concepts, and ideas.
Judging:	Settled, rules, deadlines, step-by-step instructions, careful planning, and no surprises.
Jung, Carl:	Considered the father of modern-day temperament theory.
Limbic Storm:	Uncontrolled reactions and emotions, based on childhood defenses and critical parents.
Limbic System:	Collection of brain structures that control instincts, emotions, and memories.
MBTI:	Myers-Briggs Type Indicator, a questionnaire to help determine temperament.
MBTI Code:	Four-letter combinations that represent one of 16 temperament types.
Myers, Isabel Briggs:	Daughter of Katharine Cook Briggs. Together, they created the MBTI to identify 16 specific temperaments.
Owls:	Temperament family, shares intuition and thinking (NT). *Themes: knowledge and competence.*
Perceiving:	Prefers open options, flexible rules, improvisation, spontaneity, and welcomes surprises.
Personality:	The melding of temperament and experience to create a unique individual.
Reframing:	Viewing a situation from a new angle that sheds new light and makes it more palatable.
Sensing:	Focused on reality, details and facts, practical, literal, specific, and clear.
Shaming:	Harmful name-calling or labeling.
Systems Theory:	Analyzing relationship groups using models to show interpersonal behaviors.
Supportive Counsel:	Group of real or imagined icons who provide support, counsel, criticism, and encouragement to the Vital Self.
Temperament:	The fundamental nature and instincts with which all human beings are born.
Triangling:	Any relational situation where two align against one.
Thinking:	Logical, impersonal, just, fair, notices inconsistencies, rational, and critical.
Vital Self:	The adult voice used to speak to others.

Final Thoughts ...

I

The world is better
with all of us.

II

We cannot change
others—
only ourselves.

III

We must accept
others as they are
at this very
moment.

IV

We choose
with whom we
want to associate.

V

We choose
with whom we do not
want to associate.

VI

We choose
how we will react
to others.

VII

We build
on our natural and
learned strengths.

VIII

We compensate for
our natural and learned
weaknesses.

IX

We carefully
criticize others,
mixing criticism with
affirmation.

X

We are willing and able
to laugh at ourselves.

Compiled by Larry Kidder

www.ingramcontent.com/pod-product-compliance
Lightning Source LLC
Chambersburg PA
CBHW080340290526
45791CB00009BA/2669